BRAINSTEERING

BRAINSTEERING

A BETTER APPROACH TO BREAKTHROUGH IDEAS

KEVIN P. COYNE AND SHAWN T. COYNE

HARPER
BUSINESS

An Imprint of HarperCollins*Publishers*
www.harpercollins.com

HarperCollins books may be purchased for educational, business, or sales promotional use. For information, please write: Special Markets Department, Harper-Collins Publishers, 10 East 53rd Street, New York, NY 10022.

FIRST EDITION

Designed by Renato Stanisic

Library of Congress Cataloging-in-Publication Data has been applied for.

ISBN 978-0-06-200619-6

11 12 13 14 15   OV/RRD   10 9 8 7 6 5 4 3 2 1

This book is dedicated to those we love more than we can say,
and who believed in us long before there was reason to.

FOR KEVIN
My wonderful wife, Gergana
And my three beautiful daughters, Jenny, Tricia, and Krista

FOR SHAWN
My wife, Denice (ILYSMICSI!!)
And my angels, Molly and Maria

AND FOR BOTH OF US
Our parents, Ed and Kathleen

Contents

Introduction: Why Brainsteering? 1

PART I: ASK THE RIGHT QUESTIONS (AND GOOD IDEAS WILL FOLLOW)

CHAPTER 1

The Proven Power of Questions to Help You Find Ideas 17

CHAPTER 2

Developing Your Arsenal of Right Questions 31

CHAPTER 3

When It's Time to Find a Better Idea 53

PART II: TAKE YOUR PERSONAL IDEATION SKILLS TO THE MAX

CHAPTER 4

A Systematic Approach to Developing Questions 71

CHAPTER 5

The Right (and Wrong) Uses of Analysis in Ideation 85

CHAPTER 6

Optimizing Your Personal Ideation Performance 113

PART III: LEAD OTHERS TO GREAT IDEAS

CHAPTER 7

From a Bad Brainstorming Session to a Great
Brainsteering Workshop 133

CHAPTER 8

Teaching Others to Develop Better Ideas 151

CHAPTER 9

Creating an Idea Factory 165

PART IV: THE GRAND FINALE

CHAPTER 10

Developing Your Own Billion-Dollar Idea 185

Appendix: 101 Right Questions to Spur Breakthrough Ideas 199
Acknowledgments 211
A Note on Sources 215
Notes 217
Index 225
About the Authors 239

BRAINSTEERING

Introduction

Why Brainsteering?

Don Frantz produces great shows. As a Broadway producer, he helped bring to the stage such Tony Award–winning musicals as *The Lion King* and *Beauty and the Beast*. As a producer of special events, he led the creation of such multimedia extravaganzas as the long-running SpectroMagic parade at Walt Disney World and the Dynamite Nights Stunt Spectacular at Universal Studios Florida. Super Bowl halftime shows? Been there. World's Fair exhibitions? Done that.

But perhaps none of these shows represent Mr. Frantz's most unique and successful contribution to popular culture. You see, Don Frantz is also the father of the corn maze.

That's right, you heard us. The corn maze: that now classic down-home tourist attraction that seems to appear every autumn in every community across America. The one that consistently lures your neighbors and their loved ones to spend a couple of hours trying to find their collective way through miles of twisting trails carved into acres and acres of ten-foot-tall stalks of corn.

Now, don't underestimate corn mazes. As an art form, they've been cut to resemble everything from the Seattle skyline to a portrait of Albert Einstein. And as a successful business idea—well, let's do the math. Over 600 corn mazes now appear each autumn across the landscape of the United States and Canada alone, not to mention such exotic places as China, Japan, Australia, New Zealand, Israel, Germany, and even—*sacre bleu!*—France.[1] What's more, they attract an average of about 10,000 visitors apiece (and sometimes as many as 80,000).[2] That translates to over 6 million visitors per year—which, for perspective, is nearly twice as many as the Grand Canyon or the Statue of Liberty, nearly three times as many as Mount Rushmore, and four times as many as New Orleans' famed Mardi Gras celebration.[3] In fact, it's about half the number of attendees as all the shows on Broadway *combined*. And they can all be traced back to Mr. Frantz.

So how did a Broadway producer get the idea for a corn maze? He asked himself a question. One night in 1991, he read a four-sentence press summary describing an upcoming festival of historic hedgerow mazes to be held at various English castles, and he asked himself, "What would it take to create one of these massive mazes in the United States?" The answer was far from obvious, because hedgerow mazes take many years—and are exorbitantly expensive—to grow.

Fortunately, two days later, Mr. Frantz took a whole new perspective on his question—literally. While flying cross-country on a business trip, he looked out the window, and suddenly the answer was perfectly clear. Underneath those spacious skies were mile after mile of cornfields, with row after row of tall green stalks blowing gently in the wind.

In 1993, after he and a small army of helpers spent two years asking and answering many more questions, Mr. Frantz opened the world's first corn maze on a farm in Annville, Pennsylvania. That three-acre maze, cut in the shape of an enormous dinosaur and officially designated at the time by Guinness World Records as the world's largest, attracted 11,000 visitors in just three days, raised $55,000 for farmers who had been victimized by floods earlier that year, and launched what has become a worldwide phenomenon.[4]

We all need good ideas. Breakthrough ideas. All day, every day.

In the business world, the entrepreneur or CEO needs brilliant ideas for new companies or divisions. The product manager or head of R&D needs innovative ideas for new products and services. The manufacturing manager needs practical ideas for new processes that will save time or labor and reduce costs, year after year, to keep up with the competition.

In the not-for-profit arena, the professor or teacher needs fresh ideas for her lesson plan. The student needs original ideas for his term paper. The government employee needs politically acceptable ideas for programs that will better meet the needs of her community.

And in our personal lives, we all need compelling ideas for this year's church fundraiser, or to make our twins' birthday party memorable, or to create that blockbuster movie script we've always dreamed of writing.

Some people need hundreds or thousands of ideas. That's the case for the TV producers behind those talking heads whose shows you surf past every night on cable. Every day, week after week, month after month, year after year, they have to come up with a steady stream of new and interesting story ideas that will rivet your attention and enable them to charge big bucks to their advertisers. The same dilemma faces radio talk show hosts, Web developers, advertising executives, catalog publishers, and dozens of other types of idea workers.

So how do you come up with new and better ideas all day, every day? Or even on demand? Is it really just a matter of being creative? Do some people simply have it while others don't?

No. We believe anyone can be creative. Better yet, based on fourteen years of research and consulting projects involving individuals and organizations of all shapes and sizes, we *know* anyone can be creative. Our experience shows that creative insight doesn't have to be a flash from beyond. In fact, there is a specific approach, based on proven principles and easily understood practices, that can dramatically raise your odds of consistently developing more and better ideas of almost any kind. We call this approach "Brainsteering."

Brainsteering found its beginnings in a large-scale research effort one of us led while serving as a worldwide leader of the strategy practice at the world's leading consulting firm, McKinsey & Company.

The principles and practices discovered in that research effort were used successfully in over 200 McKinsey client projects over the next few years. We have subsequently expanded upon them and applied the Brainsteering approach for a wide range of for-profit and not-for-profit clients in workshops with such diverse goals as inventing new products and services, attracting more customers, designing more efficient business processes, and reducing costs, to name just a few.

Brainsteering succeeds in virtually any setting by taking all the creative energy normally associated with traditional brainstorming and *steering* it in a more productive direction, better leveraging the way human beings actually think and work in creative problem-solving situations. It will help you tackle any kind of ideation challenge with an entirely different mindset and a whole new level of energy and curiosity. It will help you look at things from an entirely different perspective. Best of all, it will help you develop ideas you previously could never have imagined.

What's the secret to Brainsteering? As it turns out, there are two. First: if you ask the right questions, answers and good ideas soon follow. And second: the right process for consistently generating breakthrough ideas looks very different from what you've probably been taught.

Obviously, many layers of subtleties lie beneath these two simple secrets—and those layers are what this book is all about. But before we dive into those layers, perhaps you'd like a little convincing about the power of our two core principles.

ASKING THE RIGHT QUESTIONS

Let's look at the first secret of Brainsteering: *If you ask the right questions, answers and good ideas soon follow.*

How powerful can a single Right Question be? Let's visit the scene of a lunchtime discussion that took place in 1981 at a restaurant in Houston, Texas. Four years earlier, Apple Computer had legitimized the personal computer industry by introducing the Apple II, the first mass-produced personal computer. With a central processor and keyboard unit, disk drives, and a separate monitor that was about the size of a small television set, the Apple II stood about two feet tall. Transporting it required a suitcase-like box.

Then IBM followed with the IBM PC. It combined the disk drives and processor into one unit, but separated the keyboard and kept an independent monitor (also the size of a small TV). It stood about twenty-one inches tall and was heavier than the Apple. IBM allowed other manufacturers to copy its technical details, so a variety of tall, heavy machines nicknamed "PC clones" flooded the market.

In 1981, three Texas Instruments executives—Rod Canion, Bill Murto, and Jim Harris—met over lunch at a restaurant in Houston. Their discussion came to center on a single question: "How could we design an IBM-compatible computer that would fit into the overhead bin of an airplane?"[5] By the end of that lunch, the three execs had agreed on all the major design requirements—and the result was Compaq Computer Corporation, which was founded in February 1982 and grew to over a billion dollars in annual sales in less than four years—all on the strength of that one product.[6]

Was Compaq just a lucky fluke? Not at all. It's more typical than you might think. In fact, there are at least forty-one other examples just like it. Here's the story.

One of the many key subprojects during our research effort at McKinsey was to study the universe of companies that had achieved a truly extraordinary level of success: start-up companies that had grown from scratch to achieve over a billion dollars in annual revenues (measured in constant dollars as of the year 2000) in four years or less, without making a single major acquisition. We called them "Z–1–4" companies, for "zero to $1 billion within 4 years."

We found that as of 2006, there were twenty companies that had ever accomplished the Z–1–4 feat in North America, Europe, or Australia. (There may well have been others, too, but there were no comprehensive, reliable, and readily comparable data sources for effectively analyzing companies in Asia, Latin America, or Africa.) The list of megasuccessful companies included such now household names as Amazon, Reebok, Google, and of course, Compaq.

In addition, we found another twenty-three companies that we categorized as "near Z–1–4"—that is, companies that already had a modest level of annual revenues (less than $50 million) before their period of explosive growth began, or that took a little longer to reach annual revenues of nearly $1 billion (specifically, companies that took up to six years to achieve at least $850 million in annual revenues). This second group included equally famous names such as eBay, Apple, Home Depot, and Priceline.com.

Clearly, these forty-three companies would have to be considered major success stories. Although some faltered in later years for various reasons, including corporate hubris, most enjoyed continued success. And in every case, it's impossible to deny the brilliance of their early performance.

Best of all, here's the most dramatic commonality among them: *forty-two of the forty-three companies were based on a single concept.* That's right—with the exception of one company that was based on three parallel ideas, each of the Z–1–4 companies was based on a single shining idea that carried them to over a billion dollars in annual sales. Needless to say, most of them have since discovered additional ideas and grown even further—but think of the power of each company's first idea.

In many cases, the company's breakthrough idea was literally the result of answering a single specific question—the Right Question—at the outset. But much more important, we discovered that in every case, there was at least one Right Question that, had you asked it at the right time and place, could have revealed the Billion-Dollar Idea to you.

While we don't know exactly which questions the founders of all forty-two single-concept Z–1–4 companies actually asked themselves, the chart below lists several of the companies, their core idea, and a Right Question that, had you asked it at the right time and place, could have led you to the same insight.

Asking the Right Question Could Have Led You to Create These Mega Successful Companies

Z–1–4 COMPANIES, THEIR CORE IDEAS, AND POTENTIAL RIGHT QUESTIONS

Company	Core Idea	Potential Right Question
Compaq	Easily portable personal computers	How could we design an IBM-compatible computer that would fit into the overhead bin of an airplane?
Dell, Gateway	Direct sales of PCs to consumers, bypassing retail markup	Are there knowledgeable users who don't need the expensive sales support of the usual channels?
Commodore	Very inexpensive PCs for the home market	Can we still meet the needs of many users if we reduce the functionality and use older technology to reduce the cost of producing a PC by 50 percent?
Home Depot, Staples, Office Depot, Computer City, CompUSA	Large-scale ("category killer") stores for hardware, office supplies, computers	Can the "category killer" concept that Toys R Us and others used be applied to sell other types of goods?
Mannesmann Mobilfunk, Orange, E-Plus, Omnitel, DeTeMobil, Mobilcom	Cellular telephone networks in various European countries	How can we introduce into our market a new technology that has already proved commercially successful in another market (e.g., the U.S.)?
eBay	Online marketplace	How can we efficiently link passionate buyers and sellers of highly specific items who are separated from each other (in this case, by geography)?

Of course, the concept of asking the Right Question isn't limited to business ideas. In 1995, author Gregory Maguire essentially asked this question: "What might have happened in the land of Oz in the years before Dorothy dropped in via tornado?" The result was the best-selling novel *Wicked: The Life and Times of the Wicked Witch of the West*, which has sold over 4 million copies.[7] What's more, the novel was turned into the Tony Award–winning Broadway musical *Wicked*, a powerhouse show that has since gone on to break box office records all over the world, playing to over 21 million people and generating $1.7 billion in global ticket sales.[8] All because of one Right Question.

In the field of acting, one of the most important acting techniques of the twentieth century is the Method, in which actors are taught to develop their ideas for portraying the emotions called for in a particular scene by asking, "What memory do I have of experiencing an emotion comparable to one the character I am playing is experiencing?"

How about academia? Turns out there's an entire subfield of history known as "counterfactual history," which concerns itself with a single question: "What if . . . ?" (In fact, that's actually the name of one of the leading books in the field.) In counterfactual essays, historians take pivotal events and address the question "What would likely have changed if this particular event had turned out differently?" For example: "What if General Lee had been the victor, instead of the vanquished, in the Battle of Gettysburg?" Or: "What if Lee Harvey Oswald had missed?" The mind reels with possibilities.

And what about sports? In 1992, an advertising executive named Art Davie took an interest in the old sports fan's question, "Which of the martial arts is truly the most effective?" or, to put it more colloquially, "Could a black belt in karate kick the butt of a top-notch boxer?"[9] He and a few partners created Ultimate Fighting Championship 1, which was held in Denver, Colorado, on November 12, 1993 before a local stadium crowd and a pay-per-view audience of 87,000.[10] By 2007, ultimate fighting had surpassed boxing in terms of gambling revenues and set the all-time record for annual pay-per-view revenues.[11] In 2009, a single event drew a pay-per-view audience of 1.7 million people.[12]

Business. The arts. Academia. Sports. Whatever your area of interest, if you ask the Right Questions, answers—and good ideas—soon follow.

USING THE RIGHT PROCESS

Now let's turn to the second secret of Brainsteering: *The right process for consistently generating breakthrough ideas looks very different from what you've probably been taught.*

Throughout this book, we'll teach you the Right Process, a variety of fundamentally superior techniques for asking questions and more consistently creating powerful new ideas, whether you need to come up with those ideas alone or in partnership with other people. Whether in a single event or through a multistep process that takes place over time. And whether you need just one idea, or a "production line of ideas" that can turn out many good ideas each week, every week, forever.

But why do we insist that the Right Process "looks very different from what you've probably been taught" about ideation processes in the past? Well, first ask yourself whether you were ever actually taught *anything* truly useful about how to come up with great ideas in those situations where you have to work all by yourself. Virtually nothing, right? Okay, how about effective ways to create a never-ending stream of consistently innovative ideas? Again, slim pickings.

Wait! What about those situations where you can leverage the efforts of other participants (versus having to go it alone), and where you need only a single big idea (versus a constant flow)? Thank goodness you've at least been taught something for those situations! It's brainstorming, right? Everyone seems to use brainstorming—it's been a staple in creativity circles for over fifty years. But the sad truth is, traditional brainstorming actually isn't very effective.

Alex Osborn, cofounder of the legendary advertising agency Batten, Barton, Durstine & Osborn (better known as simply BBDO), first popularized the concept of brainstorming in a 1957 book entitled *Applied Imagination: Principles and Procedures of Creative Problem-Solving.* In his book, Osborn asserted that a group could produce both more and better ideas than the same number of individuals working alone. Specifically, the group would do so by "[using its collective] *brain* to *storm* a problem," and by following a list of now familiar rules such as aiming for quantity ("the greater the number of ideas, the more likelihood of winners"), thinking unconventionally ("the wilder the idea, the better—it is easier to tame down than to think up"), and accepting all ideas offered ("criticism is ruled out—adverse judgment of ideas must be withheld until later").[13] Osborn's book caused a sensation, and over the years his principles and procedures were widely adopted, sometimes in ways he intended, sometimes not, by individuals and institutions ranging from creative types on Madison Avenue to battle planners in the U.S. armed forces.

There's just one hitch. A parade of academic studies over the years have shown that traditional brainstorming is both an ineffective and inefficient technique for ideation—so much so that a leader would be better off to simply gather her team together, inform them of her ideation goals, and then send each team member off to a separate room to work alone for the same length of time that they would have spent in the group session.[14]

Surprised? If you're like the overwhelming majority of people who have regaled us over the years with stories of their own experience as participants in traditional brainstorming sessions, your answer is likely to be "Actually, come to think of it . . . no."

Why does traditional brainstorming have such a poor track record? The many causes identified in the academic literature are lengthy and complicated, but they can be summed up very succinctly: because traditional brainstorming actually violates many of the psychological and sociological principles of how human beings work best in a group setting.

As just one example of this, ask yourself, "What's the group norm when twenty people attend a meeting?" Typically, seventeen of the twenty don't say much because they just don't like speaking in large crowds, the risk of being judged by the other attendees feels too high, or they aren't confident that their idea or point of view is sufficiently valuable to take up the time of nineteen other people. While there's always a chance that three "big mouths" may think of brilliant ideas and be willing to share them with the group, 85 percent of the brainpower in the room (represented by the silent seventeen people) is usually wasted.

As another example, imagine the typical group dynamic when the highest-ranking person in the room offers—and really loves—a truly terrible idea. You know the answer: 90 percent of the time, you and everyone else just keep your heads down. After all, it usually seems better to be one of many people who allow the boss to follow a bad idea down the primrose path than the one person who declares that the emperor has no clothes and earns the boss's everlasting ire.

Think that kind of thing doesn't actually happen? We once saw the top executive in a traditional brainstorming session passionately advocate a new business in which elderly parents would prewrite birthday cards to their children, and those cards would continue to be delivered to their children every year on their birthday, long after the parents were dead. What happened? Despite being uniformly creeped out, not a single person in the room objected to the boss's idea.

So we're not only going to teach you how to find and ask the Right Questions, we're going to teach you how to use the Right Process as well, and by the time you're finished reading this book, you'll know enough about the Brainsteering approach to consistently generate breakthrough ideas in a wide variety of settings.

GETTING THE MOST OUT OF THIS BOOK

This book is organized into four parts. Each part will build on the previous one to give you an increasingly sophisticated understanding of the Brainsteering approach and prepare you for increasingly challenging ideation situations.

Part I will help you thoroughly understand why—and how—you should ask the Right Questions, enabling you to identify all kinds of powerful new ideas that might never have occurred to you in the past. If you need to create breakthrough ideas only occasionally, Part I may teach you everything you need to know.

Part II will show you how to maximize your personal ideation skills by systematically exploring every possible nook and cranny of an issue to find new ideas, and by systematically evaluating and honing your ideas as you go. These chapters can help you become an ideation superstar, the most valuable innovator in your organization.

Part III will teach you how to effectively lead others in the development of new ideas, setting the stage for your greatest ideation payoffs ever.

And speaking of payoffs, whenever you're ready to put all your newfound skills to work in the serious pursuit of an idea that could make you the founder of the next Z–1–4 company, Part IV will help you put it all together and begin developing your own Billion-Dollar Idea.

One last topic before we dive into Part I: let's talk about examples. Throughout this book, we'll use over 130 examples, large and small, to teach you both the basics and the subtle nuances of Brainsteering—and, we hope, to entertain you at the same time. Some examples will tell of incredible triumphs, others of embarrassing failures. Some will be famous examples you've read about in the *Wall Street Journal* or seen on the *Today* show. Others will be drawn from our combined fifty years of personal consulting and line management experience, as we take you behind the scenes into some of the world's best-known boardrooms (or in some cases, the world's most mind-numbingly bland conference rooms). Still others will be ideas that don't exist today, but should—examples created from scratch for the sole purpose of illustrating one principle or another as precisely as possible.

Most of the examples you'll see will describe ideas for new

things—new businesses, new products, new services, new themes, new stories. That's because we've found that people catch on to the key concepts of Brainsteering most quickly and easily when we use such examples. However, the concepts in this book can also be applied—and have been applied, quite successfully, by many of our clients—to create innovative new processes for improving everything from sales force effectiveness to debt collection efficiency; to identify new sources of valuable cost savings in everything from manufacturing expense to corporate overhead; and even to solve personal problems like finding the perfect gift for a loved one.

In fact, the Brainsteering approach works for all kinds of ideas in all kinds of environments. We've used it successfully to develop magazine columns, movie scripts, song lyrics, and themes for birthday parties. We've used it in Fortune 500 companies, tiny entrepreneurial ventures, and universities. We've used it with CEOs, sales forces, marketing gurus, finance and accounting wizards, and telephone operators. We've used it . . . well, you get the idea.

Whether you work in a for-profit or a not-for-profit organization, or all by yourself, whether you hope to apply your creative skills in the professional context of business, entertainment, or education, or in some aspect of your personal life, we hope you'll find Brainsteering to be a powerful addition to your ideation tool kit. We hope you'll find that its principles and techniques, some of which will seem counterintuitive at first, are in fact much more sensible—and effective—than other ideation principles and techniques you've been taught in the past. And in the end, we hope you'll find we've changed forever the way you think about new ideas, by steering your creative brain in a productive new direction.

PART I

ASK THE RIGHT QUESTIONS
(AND GOOD IDEAS WILL FOLLOW)

1

The Proven Power of Questions to Help You Find Ideas

Asking the Right Questions made a huge difference for Don Frantz. And for the founders of Compaq and all the Z–1–4 companies. And for all those other people we cited. But how can you be sure that a question-based approach will make such a difference for *you*?

Indulge us, if you will, in a two-part experiment. It will take less than half an hour.

First, take a quick look at your watch and block off fifteen minutes. Then put down this book and *think up a great idea for any new business you'd like*. The only constraints are that it doesn't already exist today, you haven't thought of anything like it before, and it doesn't depend on inventing any new technology (yes, teleportation travel could be quite lucrative, but for now we'll consider it off limits). Don't pick up this book again until the end of that time.

Ready? Go.

Tick-tock, tick-tock, tick-tock . . .

No, really! Go for it! Be creative! Think outside the box! What are you waiting for?

Tick-tock, tick-tock, tick-tock . . .

Okay! How did it go? Got a great idea?

If you're like most people, your answer is "No. And in fact, I really waited only five minutes because I couldn't stand it any longer."

Don't worry—even the most creative people have trouble with a completely open and unstructured directive like the one we gave you. Their minds race rapidly among various possibilities, failing to find anything they can focus their thoughts on. Before long, doubts start creeping into their minds: "Which lines of thought should I explore? Should I continue along my current line of thought or change direction altogether? How do I decide what's a good idea and what's not? How do I even decide how I'll decide? Augghhh!" Soon they start thinking about completely unrelated problems, like what time Jenny's soccer practice ends, or what to have for dinner, or which chipper young singer they're going to pull for tonight on *American Idol*. Before long, they've progressed from confusion to distraction to lethargy— and they shut down all together.

As you've probably just experienced, a completely unstructured and unconstrained approach to the task of idea generation rarely produces much. So before we ask you to take on the second part of our experiment, let's focus your mind with a question: "What do Rollerblades, Häagen-Dazs ice cream, and the *Batman* movies have in common?" We'll even give you a hint: all three are variations of the same business idea. What's that idea?

"They're all fun," you say. True, but awfully broad. We can't just ask you to develop a new business idea that's "fun" and expect you to produce a much better result than you did a few minutes ago.

"They're all things that I loved as a kid." True, sort of, but are they really just the same as when you were a kid? What you did was most likely old-fashioned roller *skating*, not newfangled Roller*blading*. You ate ice cream, but was it really as rich and sweet as Häagen-Dazs? And the *Batman* comics you read probably weren't quite as elaborate as the megaexplosions and mind-blowing chase scenes in *The Dark Knight*.

But you're getting close. In fact, building off that last observation, here's the complete answer: all three are variations of a single business concept derived from the following Right Question: "How might we take something that was emotionally powerful for people as children, then reproduce it in a more exotic—and expensive—form for adults?" Great business concept, eh? Too bad it's now been done three times, so there are no more opportunities left to take advantage of.

Or are there? Of course there are! In fact, this same concept lies behind dozens of successful products and businesses. What about $2 gourmet cookies? Or designer jelly beans that sell for $5 a pound? Ever seen those exotic $100 kites? Or $200 sneakers? Ever heard of baseball fantasy camps (or for the musically inclined, rock 'n' roll fantasy camps)? Isn't paintball just a more exotic and expensive grown-up version of playing soldiers? Ever been to a fancy corporate event where a company came in and built one of those ten-foot-tall $25,000 sand castles? What about Disney collectibles? Toy museums? Dude ranches? Any number of "adventure" vacations? Or our personal favorite, space tourism? That's right: a wealthy American businessman named Dennis Tito had the pleasure of becoming the world's first space tourist when he paid the Russian government $20 million for the privilege of spending eight days aboard the International Space Station in 2001.[1]

Want more ideas that could have sprung from that same well? Asking the "emotionally powerful as a child/expensive form for adults" question while sitting at Chuck E. Cheese (a pizza restaurant with a large arcade for kids) could logically have led to Dave and Buster's (a casual dining restaurant with a large arcade for adults). The popularity of Saturday morning cartoons directed at kids later gave rise to a host of evening cartoons directed at adults, from *The Simpsons* to *King of the Hill* to *Family Guy* to a whole host of "Adult Swim" shows. Other kid-targeted forms of entertainment like circuses and *Sesame Street* paved the way for adult-targeted versions like Cirque du Soleil and the Broadway musical *Avenue Q*.

All right, now let's do the second part of that half-hour experiment. Your task once again is to invent a new business (one that, again, does not require any new technological inventions), but this time, it must be one that takes something that was emotionally powerful to you as a child, then reproduces it in a more exotic—and expensive—form for adults.

Ready? Go.

Tick-tock, tick-tock, tick-tock . . .

How did you do this time? Better? If so, you're not alone. We've put literally thousands of people through this exercise, and the overwhelming majority of people have succeeded in creating a business concept. They've invented businesses like "fashion camps" in New York; playing cavalry commander with real army surplus tanks; cotton candy or ice cream in grown-up (read: cocktail-inspired) flavors; services that help you play hooky from work in any number of ways; and dozens of others.

When we conduct this exercise in large groups, we often split up the attendees into teams of three to five people (more later on why we specify groups of that size), then run a contest to see which team has developed the "best idea." Teams who wish to participate in the contest bid against each other (using money from their own wallets) for the right to be one of four teams who will be given the opportunity to present their idea to the whole gathering. The top-bidding teams put their money into a pot, and in return they're given one minute to make their pitch. All the attendees then vote to determine the "best idea," and the winning team claims the entire jackpot. And what usually happens? First, the majority of teams like their idea enough that they enter the bidding. Second, many teams like their idea so much that they bid up to $100 just for the right to present. And third, we occasionally have teams who refuse to reveal their idea at all, because they intend to actually pursue it.

Why did you likely succeed in the second round of this experiment, when you might have failed—or bailed—in the first? Because we helped you steer your creativity in a productive direction. The Right Question provided you with just enough of a constraint to help you focus, or "anchor," your thinking. Instead of bouncing around randomly, you were enabled—in fact, forced—to more fully explore a carefully defined subset of the possible universe. And because you stuck with that single Right Question for several minutes, you were able to take your initial ideas, which were probably only so-so, and keep massaging them until one or more of them evolved into a good one, or even a great one. "That idea won't work," you probably thought, "but maybe *this* one would." Or "That idea wouldn't work under those circumstances, but it *would* work under these other circumstances."

All thanks to the Right Question.

Ironic, isn't it? One of the classic "creativity" mantras we've all heard repeatedly over the years—"Free yourself completely and think outside the box!"—turns out to be precisely the wrong advice. People actually tend to perform worse, not better, when they're given no constraints at all (as in, "Think up a great idea for any new business you'd like"). As it turns out, you're more likely to succeed by thinking *inside* a box—the key is to find just the right box in which to think.

Need a second demonstration to *really* convince you? Maybe you'd like to see how a single Right Question can lead to an idea for a "serious" new business—none of that grown-up kid stuff. Maybe you'd like to see an idea for a business that should exist but doesn't.

In the earliest days of developing the Brainsteering approach, we were charged with finding an important innovation for one of the world's largest gasoline retailers, a company that owns thousands of gas stations and convenience stores across the United States and around the world. Frankly, the gasoline retailing business is a difficult one: profit margins are slim, competition is fierce, and it's gotten even worse in recent years as large grocery chains and warehouse stores have entered the market with cut-throat pricing. (Twenty years ago, gasoline stations added convenience stores and siphoned off the high-margin snack business from grocery stores. Now, in what must be some form of karmic payback, grocery stores have learned to price gasoline low in order to steal back customers from the convenience stores.)

We asked ourselves questions—lots of questions. The breakthrough came when we asked, "What is the single biggest hassle that a customer puts up with in purchasing gasoline?" We started out thinking incrementally—things like getting their hands dirty, getting out of the car on a cold or rainy day, and so on. Then we thought more broadly: actually, the biggest hassle is having to go get gasoline at all.

At first, this insight led to an unhelpful detour (one that we'll teach you to avoid later), as we discussed ideas like electric cars and hydrogen-based cars. But soon we realized that those inventions wouldn't really eliminate the hassle factor; they would only change its form. For example, instead of driving to a gas station and hooking a gas pump to your car, you'd have to drive to a hydrogen station and hook a hydrogen pump to your car.

Then it hit us: The biggest *addressable* hassle was having to go to a gas station to purchase gasoline. After all, the average car sits around doing nothing about 95 percent of the time. (Driving a typical 15,000 miles a year at an average speed of 35 miles per hour takes 429 hours, or about 5 percent of the total hours in a year.) How could that idle time be used to fill up the car with gas?

The answer came instantly: *Bring the gas to the car.* Imagine a fleet of cheerfully logo'd, friendly looking pickup-truck-sized vehicles—miniature gasoline tankers resembling those familiar TruGreen Chem-Lawn trucks that cruise through suburban neighborhoods each day to spray fertilizer on the lawns of McMansions. Now imagine each mini-tanker being driven by a courteous uniformed attendant who could service your car right where it's parked.

Of course this idea, like most ideas, wouldn't work everywhere. One problem for the vendor would be overcoming the inherent inefficiency of driving around searching for cars needing to be filled. Another would be the difficulty of handling cash or one-off credit card transactions. And, importantly, would anyone really want to sit around in his car waiting for the truck to come by? That would defeat the entire purpose of the service.

Yes, there are problems, but the idea just feels like something consumers could get excited about, doesn't it? Something that could be made feasible under certain conditions? So your restless mind automatically begins generating the next round of relevant questions. For example: "Where and when are there consistently going to be many cars parked right next to each other for long periods of time? So many cars that, even if only one in ten or one in twenty needs gas that day, the next customer's car is easy for my truck driver to find and only a very short distance from the car he just filled?"

We know your mind is already racing ahead with potential solutions to the questions above, and probably with further helpful questions as well. But to find out what happens, you'll have to wait until we return to this story in Chapter 5.

So the Right Question can lead to some great ideas, both whimsical and serious. But that's not enough. We promised you that Brainsteering would enable you to consistently develop more and better ideas of all kinds. To fulfill that promise, the Right Question technique must address two additional concerns you might have:

> What if the best Right Question I can think of has been used before?
> What if I never think of the perfect Right Question—am I
> doomed to think of only mediocre ideas?

Let's address each of these concerns in turn.

WHAT IF THE BEST RIGHT QUESTION I CAN THINK OF HAS BEEN USED BEFORE?

Many people worry that, because their particular type of challenge has been around for a long time, there are no new ideas to be found. Similarly, they worry that there are no new Right Questions to be asked, that "all the best ones have been taken."

Don't worry. Every person has different experiences and different thought patterns. Therefore, asking three different people the identical question, even in the identical situation, almost always elicits three different ideas. As long as the Right Question is new to *you*, don't worry if others have already asked it somewhere in the past.

To illustrate, would you believe that the exact same Right Question led to major breakthroughs in two fields as different from each other as jet engines and gingerbread houses? It did. The question was "What other items or activities that are highly related to those of my current product could my product be modified to take advantage of?"

In the case of jet engines, the answers in 1982 were "fuel" and "maintenance." First, fuel was obviously a major expense; anything the engine control system could do to save fuel would be extremely valuable. Second, if an engine needed emergency repairs at an airport where an airline didn't have the proper facilities, those repairs were far more expensive, so predicting future breakdowns would be hugely valuable.

When jet engines began to be controlled by onboard computers in the early 1980s, United Technologies discovered that an engine's computers could be programmed to both improve fuel efficiency *and* remember a whole host of data regarding its performance during each flight. That data could then be used to predict the engine's future need for repairs, enabling the airline to schedule those repairs on a routine basis at a properly equipped facility. Based on the simultaneous savings achieved in both fuel efficiency and maintenance costs, United Technologies was soon able to raise the price of its engines.[2]

As for gingerbread houses, the time was 1993. For nearly a century, the Grove Park Inn of Asheville, North Carolina, had been a leading resort in the spring, summer, and fall seasons, but had remained closed during the winter. In recent years, it had begun staying open during the winter months, but it wasn't attracting nearly enough visitors. Worse yet, its decorating budget had dwindled over the years, so it didn't have the option of spending massively on seasonal decorations.

But one day, James Craig Madison, then the inn's marketing manager and now its CEO, essentially asked himself a modified version of the same Right Question that United Technologies had asked: "What other items or activities that are highly related to those of my current product could my product be modified to take advantage of?" In Grove Park Inn's case, the question became "What popular activities go with Christmas that no other resort has already exploited, but that I could inexpensively modify my calendar of winter events to take advantage of?"

His answer: Grove Park Inn could create and host a major gingerbread house–building competition.[3] Competitors would be one source of revenue, and visitors drawn by the chance to see these unique works of art would be an even larger one. The competition was a huge success, and it now draws over 300 entrants per year from all over the nation—along with thousands of visitors. The winner of the competition is now featured nationally each year on ABC's *Good Morning America*, and the Grove Park Inn consistently maintains high occupancy throughout the entire Christmas season.[4] All because Mr. Madison recognized a connection between Christmas and gingerbread houses that other hotels didn't.

So don't worry that someone else has used your Right Question before. Use it anyway. (In fact, in Chapter 2, we're going to tell you to actively collect questions that have already been used in situations similar to yours.)

For further proof that a single Right Question can be used over and over, let's return to a question we explored earlier: "What's the biggest hassle a customer has to deal with [in my area of interest]?" That question has been asked—and very successfully answered—in many industries.

For customers of the U.S. Postal Service, the biggest hassle associated with buying stamps used to occur whenever first-class rates went up. Remember how it seemed you were always going back to buy additional one- or two-cent stamps? Or those times when you couldn't recall whether rates had risen since you last bought a book of stamps and you sat, paralyzed, trying to decide whether to drive to the post office or just risk it? Thinking about those hassles led our friends at the USPS to invent the Forever Stamp, the stamp that will cover the postage for a first-class letter whenever it is used in the future, regardless of what level the rate may have risen to by that time.

In the used car business, the top three customer hassles used to be haggling over price; having to traipse from place to place to see more than one vehicle of the type you wanted; and worrying that the car you were about to buy contained hidden defects. Enter CarMax, which revolutionized the used car business with fixed pricing (no more haggling), huge lots (goodbye, selection hassle), and both a five-day money-back guarantee and a thirty-day limited warranty (ahhh, peace of mind).

Importantly, you can expect to produce new and innovative ideas by reusing a Right Question even in those cases where someone else has already applied the exact same question in the exact same situation.

Take air travel hassles. At the highest level, a large portion of the private jet industry exists because the biggest hassle many executives want to avoid is the entire airport experience. Don't believe the old line that says private jets are justified on the basis that they save senior executives a lot of time when traveling to remote locations. Our senior clients don't use their jets just to get in and out of airports that aren't conveniently serviced by commercial airlines; they use them even when there are direct flights available. In addition, they don't use their jets because they're more comfortable to ride in, because private jets aren't really more comfortable. Most corporate jets are so small that you can't even stand up straight as you squeeze your way down the aisle; have seats that are no wider than those on commercial jets; and feature bathrooms located so close to the other seats that any illusion of privacy requires a true suspension of disbelief. No, the real reason so many executives use private jets is simply to avoid the hassle of the entire airport experience. And if we were rich enough, we would, too.

Alas, for the vast majority of passengers—including us—avoiding the airport experience is simply not an option. Therefore, a few airlines go to great lengths to at least minimize the hassle. Virgin Atlantic has created over-the-top waiting lounges in several airports to reduce the stress of the airport experience. And many airlines have taken the less dramatic (but still helpful) step of paying extra fees to selected airports to create priority access lines that help speed their high-value passengers through security checkpoints. To help all passengers reduce the hassle of the airport experience, most airlines offer the ability to check in and print boarding passes online. And nearly all airlines provide automated touch screen check-in kiosks that help most passengers check in quickly while also reducing the waiting lines for those people who need to speak directly with a representative.

Same question, same situation—yet many different ideas. So don't feel like you have to find a question that's never been asked before; all you have to do is find a great question that *you've* never asked before.

WHAT IF I NEVER THINK OF THE PERFECT RIGHT QUESTION? AM I DOOMED TO THINK OF ONLY MEDIOCRE IDEAS?

When we first developed the principles and techniques that later grew into the Brainsteering approach, we were haunted by the same doubt. We erroneously thought there might be a set of "magic" questions that were somehow better than all other possible questions. But if that were true, then the task of finding the perfect question could prove as difficult as finding the breakthrough idea itself through some other method. And what good would that be?

Our problem—and yours—was solved accidentally when we began trying to guess what questions might have led to the kind of Z–1–4 company ideas that we showed you in the introduction. We found that for any given Z–1–4 company's core idea, each member of our team had a different guess regarding the question that produced it, but all of our guesses could have produced the idea. Translation: there were multiple paths to the same great idea.

Later, the multiple-paths-to-the-same-great-idea phenomenon was reinforced for us through another set of work. As we expanded our lists of Right Questions (which we'll teach you to do in Chapter 4), we constantly looked for real-life "signpost examples" of great ideas that could have come from each question. We found ourselves arguing, because some examples just seemed to be the perfect answer to several Right Questions. But soon we realized, once again, that we'd found multiple paths to the same great idea.

Let's illustrate this phenomenon with a well-known success story from the consumer services market: Jiffy Lube. Although it has expanded its range of services over the years, Jiffy Lube's early massive success was predicated on a single service offering: fast, inexpensive oil changes provided on a drive-through, no-reservations-required basis. From its founding in 1979, Jiffy Lube grew to over 1,000 locations before selling out to Pennzoil in 1990—and today the company's bright red signs can be seen in over 2,000 locations.[5]

According to cofounder Stephen Spinelli: "So many people have told me that they thought of the Jiffy Lube idea first, but they didn't do anything with it."[6] Do you think all those people asked themselves the identical question? Obviously not.

The fact is, you could have discovered the Jiffy Lube idea by asking yourself any of several questions about the various services performed on cars by full-service garages and the service departments of auto dealerships:

For what portion of the services is the current system [of full-service garages] least well suited? This question would have caused you to examine the fact that those garages are staffed by expensive, highly trained mechanics whose skills are far beyond that required to simply change the oil in a car. Or it might have caused you to identify how messy performing an oil change can be, and how cleaning up oil spills is time consuming and expensive for a full-service garage.

Which customers don't need the full set of capabilities that we charge our customers for? Full-service garages typically break down charges into "parts" and "labor." They cover all their other expenses (like equipment and utilities) by calculating the entire expense of their operation (excluding parts), then dividing it by their total number of labor hours to determine what price per hour to charge for "labor." That's why you see such high labor rates (often $50 to $100 per labor hour) posted in full-service garages and the service departments of auto dealerships. But if the only thing Jiffy Lube planned to do was change oil, it didn't need most of the expensive equipment required to outfit a full-service garage. Therefore, it could be far more cost efficient, and charge far lower prices, even if its mechanics took just as long to change a car's oil as the mechanics at a full-service garage.

What's the biggest (avoidable) hassle customers face? Under the old system, a customer usually had to schedule an oil change just as far in advance as a major repair, because most shops worked on a first-in, first-out basis. Further, a customer often had to leave her car at the shop for the day, because even though a simple oil change could actually be accomplished very quickly, any time overruns on earlier cars' repairs or services could prevent the available mechanics from getting to her simple oil change. These hassles could be avoided *if* the only services provided were ones that could be finished quickly. In that case, it would be much easier to offer drive-through, no-reservations-required service and much more accurate estimates of how long the customer would have to wait.

Where have changes in the competitive landscape left some customers poorly served, relative to the past? Always a great question to ask. In fact, an indirect insight along this very line of inquiry was the actual genesis of Jiffy Lube. You see, in the late 1970s, a man named James Hindman learned that the number of full-service garages had fallen by half during the previous ten years. Most had been replaced by self-service gas stations, which meant that millions of customers had lost the place where they normally took their cars for oil changes. Before long, Mr. Hindman partnered with Mr. Spinelli and another man named Ed Kelley, and the rest is history.[7]

The bottom line is, you don't have to labor under the crushing belief that you must find the perfect question. There are multiple paths to the same great idea.

One last thing before we move on to Chapter 2, something that may be gnawing at you: *If asking the Right Questions is so powerful, why hasn't anyone pointed this out before?* Some people have, just not quite so directly. In fact, the practice of asking Right Questions actually dates back at least to 400 B.C., when according to his star pupil Plato, the Greek philosopher Socrates developed what was then called *elenchus*, or what we know today as the "Socratic method."

When you use the Socratic method, you break down a problem into a series of questions, the answers to which gradually distill the solution. Socrates' approach was somewhat similar to ours, but its focus was on the negative: a person would form a number of hypotheses to be tested, then subject them to a series of questions and eliminate those that led to contradictions. The expectation was that new and better hypotheses would gradually be identified, until at last one answer stood up under all the scrutiny, at which point the problem would be considered solved. The Right Question approach works much the same way, except that its focus is on the positive, and (warning: bad pun ahead) we're "positive" that it can work for you.

So, if you ask the Right Questions, answers—and good ideas— soon follow. Which begs yet another question: "How do I find the Right Questions?"

2

Developing Your Arsenal of Right Questions

If asking the Right Questions is critical, then the most critical question of all is, "How do I find the Right Questions?"

We're going to tell you—but before you can begin searching for Right Questions, there's another question to be answered first: "How will I recognize a Right Question when I see one?" Fortunately, there are four simple criteria.

A RIGHT QUESTION FORCES YOU TO TAKE A PERSPECTIVE YOU HAVEN'T TAKEN BEFORE

When people look for new ideas to attack the same type of problem they've attacked before—say, developing the next version of a software package, or identifying the next round of cost savings in a manufacturing plant, or coming up with the next theme for the marching band's annual fund-raiser—they tend to fall into patterns. They repeat the same line of inquiry that's been successful for them in the past. This is a losing strategy, because if you keep going down the same path, you'll find it harder and harder to think of something new.

This phenomenon, which you've probably experienced yourself, has also been clearly confirmed in rigorous studies. In his ground-breaking book *Innovation: The Attacker's Advantage*, Richard Foster examined the relationship between the mental effort required to develop an innovation (as measured by R&D hours) and the resulting effectiveness of the innovation itself (such as a new technology, product, or process).[1] If you draw a graph plotting mental effort on the horizontal axis and effectiveness on the vertical axis, you'll see a relationship that looks like an S-curve.

If you keep going down the same path, you'll find it harder and harder to think of something new

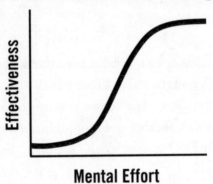

Figure 2.1: Innovation "S-Curve"

The slope of the curve starts out very flat. It takes a lot of effort to produce even small improvements in effectiveness, as the potential inventor tends to flounder a bit at first. He makes a lot of mistakes and explores a lot of pathways that turn out to be dead ends—because he doesn't yet know what's truly important. (In our case, this might represent the time you spend developing useless or irrelevant questions before finding any *good* questions.)

If the inventor hangs in there, the flat slope begins to turn sharply upward as he hits on the key elements necessary to improve effectiveness (or in our case, as you find the first few Right Questions and begin to work with them). For a while, the insights come fast and furious, and the slope continues dramatically upward as the inventor gains traction.

But after a while, the slope begins to flatten out again, meaning that more and more mental effort is required to squeeze out fewer and/ or smaller gains in effectiveness. This corresponds to the situation we described above, in which most people tend to repeat the same line of inquiry and return to the same questions again and again. Generally speaking, Mr. Foster tells us, the slope never turns upward again. It just keeps getting flatter and flatter.

In fact, in this part of the curve, it's even possible to predict just how hard it will be to find the next improvement in effectiveness—and the mathematics paint a daunting picture. Let's say you've just worked ten hours to find a 3 percent improvement in effectiveness. The formulas predict that the next 3 percent gain will require twenty hours of additional work. Another 3 percent? That will take you forty hours. Then eighty. Then 160. And so on. Just thinking about it kind of wears you out, doesn't it?

You can readily see how people get trapped. They develop an approach that works really well—once, twice, even three or four times. Then one day it works again, but only pretty well. "That's okay," they tell themselves, "maybe I'm just having an off day." The next time they need an improvement, they're working on a deadline, so they're afraid to risk trying something new and they use it again. It's a grind, but they muddle through and eventually produce a decent idea—so they hang on to their crutch, even though it's getting more and more painful to use.

Bottom line: people who try to come up with good ideas by constantly assembling the same team and approaching the same problem from the same perspective, time after time, must devote exponentially more effort each time they need an improvement. In contrast, a question that forces you to take a new perspective will temporarily burden you with some intense start-up effort, but will soon reward you with stronger insights and better ideas, and will keep doing so for a good while thereafter.

A RIGHT QUESTION LIMITS THE CONCEPTUAL SPACE YOU EXPLORE

This one often strikes people as being counterintuitive, but as we demonstrated in Chapter 1, most people actually perform worse when "thinking outside the box" than when they are "thinking inside a [carefully designed] box." That's because, when someone asks a group to "think outside the box" and places no limits on the conceptual space to be explored, there are simply too many possible directions in which to go. People's minds race, first in one direction, then in another. "Let's make it bigger (or smaller)!" Or "Let's sell it over there (or there, or there)!" Or "Let's make it ten times less expensive (or ten times more expensive)!" Or . . . or . . . or. It's impossible to gain much traction, or even to know whether any particular direction represents a step forward or a step backward. Under these circumstances, people generally shut down fairly quickly (and often resist participating in future idea-generation exercises as well). But as we demonstrated with the "emotionally powerful as a child/expensive form for adults" example, the opposite happens when there's a focusing device like a question.

Expressed in terms of the Innovation S-curve, trying to cover too much conceptual space dooms you to spending only a little bit of time exploring any one part of that space. As a result, you continually flounder around at the bottom of the S-curve for many parts of that space, and never move up the curve for any one of them.

EVEN THOUGH A RIGHT QUESTION LIMITS THE CONCEPTUAL SPACE YOU EXPLORE, IT MUST STILL PROVIDE LOTS OF HIGHLY ATTRACTIVE POSSIBILITIES

If the question is so narrow that there is only one obvious and dominant answer, then the question won't work; it will shut down people's thinking instead of enhancing it. 'Nuff said.

A RIGHT QUESTION JUST PLAIN SUCCEEDS

Just as some innovations are simply better than others—that is, they have taller S-curves—some questions are simply better than others.

Just run a quick sanity check: If a question immediately makes you think of more than one intriguing possibility, then it's likely to help other people produce even more possibilities if you use it more extensively. In contrast, if a question fails to stimulate a single useful train of thought right away, it's probably a dud.

Four simple criteria, and now you can spot a Right Question from a mile away. So let's begin developing that arsenal.

Ponder for a moment the achievements of Albert Einstein or Pablo Picasso. They each sought an insight that might occur once in a thousand lifetimes. To do so, they each had to find, ask, and answer questions that no one had ever thought of. That's why their searches encompassed years, decades, or even lifetimes. They each spent an unusually long time finding the Right Questions to ask—but when they found them, their ideas were revolutionary and their success was unparalleled.

The good news for you? Your task isn't nearly as difficult. You see, for the vast majority of us, in the vast majority of the situations we encounter, the problem-solving and ideation challenges we face fit into patterns—and therefore so do the Right Questions. Consequently, you can "borrow" Right Questions from those who came before you. After all, you aren't the first person who's ever had to identify an original strategy for entering a new market, or improve your product in response to competitive pressures, or find a fresh approach to a charity fund-raiser.

Let's say you want to invent a new business or product. You could start by borrowing the questions that led to some of the most successful business and product launches in history and adapting them to your particular circumstances. A bit earlier, we saw that Compaq Computer Corporation grew out of a single question, the more generalized version of which is: "Who has a significant need for this kind of product, but is prevented from buying or using it because of one key obstacle?"

That question focused the thinking of an Englishman named

Trevor Baylis in 1991 after he watched a TV show about AIDS in Africa. According to Mr. Baylis, "The programme said that the big problem was getting the health message across. Broadcasts on safe sex were not reaching many areas. In remote villages, there was no electricity, and the cost of batteries [for] radios was prohibitive."[2]

There it was: the key obstacle. Or in his case, two key obstacles. (Which reminds us to offer the following advice: Don't get trapped by taking the wording of anyone else's Right Question too literally— remember to borrow *and adapt*.)

Now that Mr. Baylis had zeroed in on the critical issues, a breakthrough idea came to him (as he put it himself) "in a flash of inspiration. I imagined someone listening close to the horn of an old gramophone. It was obvious: if a clockwork gramophone could produce that sound, why not apply the idea to a radio?" Bingo. Baylis invented a wind-up radio. The user simply turns a crank on the outer case of the radio, which winds up the mainspring inside. That mainspring powers a small electrical generator that, in turn, powers the radio. Naturally, much hard work and many unsuccessful prototypes followed, but Mr. Baylis's wind-up radio, branded as the Freeplay, reached the market in South Africa in 1995. Millions of Freeplay radios have since been sold, and Mr. Baylis has received a dozen honorary doctorates as well as the Order of the British Empire from the queen of England.[3]

While the lessons and ideas spawned by others who came before you may not solve your entire problem, they can certainly give you a substantial jump-start on it by being the source of great questions that help you focus your thinking. So constantly add to your arsenal by looking at other people's successes and asking yourself, "What's the question that—if I had asked it in that time and place—would likely have led me to the answer they found?" And keep reminding yourself that it doesn't matter if others have used a great question before, because a great question generates many possibilities. Remember, nobody stopped asking the "emotionally powerful as a child/expensive form for adults" question just because someone else had already invented Rollerblades, or created Häagen-Dazs ice cream, or shot a *Batman* movie. Instead, a lot of nobodies became somebodies by inventing the dozens of other products and services that could result from that question.

Over the years, we've collected hundreds of Right Questions, some highly original, and some that are variants of each other. The appendix to this book contains 101 of them. A close look at our list reveals certain patterns. In particular, the following five lines of inquiry almost always pay off:

Identifying unsolved customer problems
"De-averaging" users and activities
Exploring unexpected successes
Imagining perfection
Discovering unrecognized "headroom"

To illustrate the power of these lines of inquiry, let's review some specific sample questions, complete with real-life signpost examples of the inventions and ideas they could have spawned.

IDENTIFYING UNSOLVED CUSTOMER PROBLEMS

Customers always have problems. The easiest category of high payoff questions lies in finding original ways to identify and categorize those problems.

What's the biggest (avoidable) hassle customers face? As we discussed in detail in the last chapter, this question could lead to Forever Stamps, Jiffy Lube, Internet-based check-in for airlines, and private jets.

For which users, or which occasions, are current products least well suited? In 1981, Mike Sinyard was running a tiny bicycle parts company. One day he noticed that he was selling a lot of unusual parts to a small group of biking enthusiasts in Marin County, California, near San Francisco. He discovered that these riders were freewheeling down mountain trails on makeshift bicycles (referred to as "klunkers") that combined a frame from the 1930s for geometry and strength, retrofitted brakes and tires, additional gears, and motocross handlebars. To better meet the needs of such riders, Mr. Sinyard created the first mass-produced mountain bike, which he dubbed the "Specialized Stumpjumper." When mountain biking took off in the mid-1980s, so did Mr. Sinyard's company. Today, Specialized Bike Components is a top brand, with sales of $500 million per year.[4]

Based on that same question, here's a product that doesn't exist, but should. On what occasion is it most miserable to be in your car? When you first start it up on an ice-cold morning, right? Don't you hate feeling like a caged icicle? But of course, the car's heater works off the engine block, so it takes ages to warm up. And if you try turning up the heater to nudge the process along, it just blows more cold air on you in the meantime. So why couldn't cars be equipped with the equivalent of miniature space heaters, supplemental devices that would provide virtually instant heat and work off the car's alternator until the engine block warms up?

What group of potential customers is as large as the industry's current customer base, but doesn't buy our product or service for one particular [addressable] reason? How many older persons (and younger technophobes) avoid computers because they don't really understand how the programs work? These people are actually put off by the scads of features built into most popular programs. While geeks might appreciate that Microsoft Word allows the user to change the font, change the color, adjust the margins, highlight, center the text, add pictures and graphs, and so on, to the neophyte these options just look like complexity. They represent a hundred more ways for the computer to suddenly do something that the user doesn't want and doesn't know how to fix.

Now imagine there was a line of software called Radically Simple, a convenient line of programs that overlay the most popular software programs and present extremely simplified interfaces. They accomplish this by hiding from the user 95 percent or more of the "fancier" (read: arguably unnecessary) options built into the underlying programs. With fewer options to present on the screen, the buttons can be larger, and can actually say what they do, instead of illustrating what they do via hieroglyphics that the novice user can't understand. And they can appear right there on the surface versus being hidden in drop-down boxes. The result? A whole new market segment for computers.

DE-AVERAGING USERS AND ACTIVITIES

In most idea-generation processes, there's a lot of attention paid to averages. "What's the average age of our customers? How many times per year, on average, do they use our product or service? What's the average price they pay?"

The purpose of this group of questions is to "*de*-average" your users and their activities. To look for outliers. To find those cases where your product or service may have been designed and delivered to meet the average needs of average customers in average situations, but where there is already evidence—hidden within existing sales or usage patterns—that uncovers useful variations in your customers and/or their behavior.

Who uses our product/service in surprisingly large quantities—and why? Here, the emphasis should be on the word "surprisingly." Otherwise, the question is likely to prompt an unimaginative discussion about how the company should reward its largest customers, and the session will devolve into proposing yet another version of loyalty programs.

Further, "surprisingly" means avoiding patterns and concentrations that the company already knows about. A fast food company already knows that over 30 percent of its volume comes from people who eat more than twenty meals a month at its restaurants. A liquor company already knows that a huge portion of its volume is sold to people who the Centers for Disease Control and Prevention classify as "problem drinkers." Don't waste your time on known patterns. Look for the surprises—the *un*known patterns.

In the 1970s, a Harvard Business School case told of one baby food company that found its sales in Florida were vastly out of proportion to the number of babies in Florida. Why did Floridian babies eat so much baby food compared to similarly cute and cuddly cherubs in other states? No one seemed to know. But the variance from national averages was so significant that it could represent a huge opportunity for the company if it could be replicated elsewhere, so it was worth the effort to find out. Eventually, the company's key manager in Florida divulged the secret: senior citizens. The extra baby food wasn't being consumed by babies at all; it was being consumed by older persons, many of them living in condos and retirement homes, who desired small portions of nutritious foods that could be consumed easily even if they had lost their teeth. That finding led to a whole new product line for the company.

Flash forward to the millennium in Japan. From a peak of $252 million in 1999, baby food sales fell to $235 million in 2001. As one story on BusinessWeek.com put it, "Confronted with a steady drop in the number of newborns, baby food makers were on the lookout for a new source of revenue when they stumbled on an intriguing trend. . . . Already, one out of every five Japanese is sixty-five or older; by 2014, it'll be one out of four." Once again, senior citizens were targeted—but the baby food makers were very careful in how they marketed their new product. Back to BusinessWeek.com: "[One company] sells its elder food as 'Fun Meals,' while [another] labels its pouches 'Food for Ages 0–100.' 'Nobody wants to buy food for geezers,' said Satoshi Inagaki of the Japan Babyfood Assn."[5]

Which customers does our industry prefer not to serve, and why? There are often great opportunities to be capitalized upon by finding ways to serve the customer nobody else wants. Progressive Insurance, now one of America's largest auto and property insurers, first rose to prominence by capturing the "substandard auto market"—that is, by being willing to insure drivers with bad claims histories, precisely the kind of drivers that other companies didn't want to serve. Similarly, the banking industry has allowed several major categories of financial services providers to develop that focus on customers it didn't want to serve. Consider check cashing and payday loan providers, both of which have grown to be multibillion-dollar, highly profitable categories that the banks could have dominated were they not trapped by their own prejudices.

EXPLORING UNEXPECTED SUCCESSES

Here, the focus shifts even more toward fringe customers and users and their behavior. There may not be a discernible volume of unusual customers behaving unusually just yet (so the previous questions might miss them), but only because other *potential* fringe users haven't found out yet about those customers and their behaviors. To uncover such instances, just ask your questions a little differently.

Who uses our product/service in ways we never expected or intended? Take sodium bicarbonate, more commonly known as baking soda. In 1846, two bakers named John Dwight and Austin Church built their first factory in Mr. Dwight's kitchen to produce this highly useful chemical that helps dough rise. Their brand, Arm & Hammer, soon became the dominant brand of sodium bicarbonate, and generations of consumers happily used it for baking. But eventually, consumers found other uses for it. They placed open boxes in their iceboxes to absorb odors. They used it to freshen their laundry. They used it to brush their teeth. Alternative uses of baking soda eventually became commonly cited household tips in women's magazines. As a result, in the 1970s, the company began to actively market what eventually became an entire family of

Arm & Hammer products, including laundry detergent, toothpaste, underarm deodorant, and cat litter. Today, the use of Arm & Hammer baking soda by consumers for baking—the original basis on which the entire company was founded—represents such a small percentage of the company's sales that its 2008 10K Annual Report neglected to even specify "consumer baking" in the SEC-required description of the company's business.[6]

How about this example? In China, there's a famous story about washing machines. It seems that Haier Corporation, China's largest appliance manufacturer, was experiencing difficulties with its washing machines in Szechuan province. Depending on which version of the story you read, the problem was either unusually poor sales, frequent breakdowns of its machines, or both. Upon investigation, Haier discovered that the local peasant farmers were using the washing machines to wash *sweet potatoes*—and needless to say, the machines were having a rough time with the task.[7] Local agents suggested an education campaign to teach the locals that the machines were for clothes—but instead, the higher-ups decided to augment the machine's design. According to one report, three days of design drawings resulted in a machine that captured half the market.[8] (Sadly, we have found no documentation regarding what products account for the *other* half of the sweet potato washing machine market.)

Want one more? Let's talk about traveler's checks in South America. Before consumers had universal access to ATMs, traveler's checks were a major product in the financial services industry. The value of traveler's checks over cash was that if they were lost or stolen, the issuer would refund the traveler's money. Customers would buy the checks from a financial institution (also paying a fee) and carry them on their trip. Stores would accept the checks, then turn them in to their own banks in exchange for cash. Those banks would then cash in the checks at the original issuer and receive a fee from the issuer for having accepted them. The issuer made money two ways: from the fees it charged travelers (minus the fees it paid to the banks that had accepted the checks), and from the interest it earned between the time the travelers bought the checks (and turned over cash to the issuer) and the time the accepting banks presented the checks for payment (at which time the issuer had to turn over the cash to the accepting banks). The issuing institutions encouraged travelers to keep some checks in their wallet at all times, just in case. Of course, those were the most profitable checks of all, because they might sit uncashed in a traveler's wallet for months.

Actually, in certain cases, those were only the *second* most profitable checks. You see, because the government reporting requirements for bank transactions involving traveler's checks were less stringent than for those involving regular cash, traveler's checks became an alternative currency among drug lords in South America—and those checks remained uncashed for *years*.

IMAGINING PERFECTION

Have you ever gotten frustrated at the limitations of the world around you? Have you ever imagined what the world would be like if a product existed that would completely solve your particular problem, versus making it only marginally less painful? You know, the real science fiction stuff, like the time you daydreamed that your car could simply levitate above that monster traffic jam and whisk you off to your destination? Or that you could press your thumbprint into a little box at the top of some lengthy medical form and have it automatically fill in all the medical history details you've already provided to dozens of doctors in the past?

Well, the questions in this category are the ones where you get to put that kind of imagination to work. They're all variants of this question: "What if the world (or at least a certain corner of it) were perfect?"

Consider this real-life example in which a single person revolutionized a sport that had existed for over a hundred years: competitive swimming. In high school, David Berkoff was a good swimmer, but—by his own admission—certainly not world class. However, in 1985, during his freshman year at Harvard, he asked himself a question: "Why don't we swim more like the best swimmers on the planet—that is, fish?" (Or, as he later clarified, dolphins, whose underwater swimming motion can be more easily mimicked by humans than that of fish, whose tails typically flutter from side to side. Next time you're in a swimming pool, try fluttering your body from side to side and you'll instantly understand the value of Mr. Berkoff's clarification.)

Young Mr. Berkoff played around with new kicking motions after practice a few times. Then came his opportunity. The Harvard coaches had scheduled a kind of preseason intrasquad meet, the primary purpose of which seems to have been for the upperclassmen to prove their innate superiority over the freshmen. When it was Mr. Berkoff's turn to race, he dove in and swam the first fifteen meters completely underwater, kicking like a dolphin with his entire lower body—"just to be a goof," he told us, "but then I looked back and saw that I had just smoked everyone."

As always, a lot of work followed in order to refine his innovation. "I had to completely change my training to increase the speed and endurance of my kicks, and to help my body adjust to being in a hypoxic state [that is, the state of oxygen deprivation caused by staying underwater for so long]. I started trying it in competition, and I would get huge leads at first, but then I'd run out of gas and lose at the end. I had to train for a while before my body got used to it."

But the idea was born, and before long it paid off—big-time. In 1986, Mr. Berkoff placed third in the 100-meter backstroke at the NCAA finals. In 1987, he finished first in the 100-meter backstroke, and did it in NCAA record time. The next year, at the U.S. Olympic trials, he broke the world record—twice. A month and a half later, he broke it again at the 1988 Olympics in Seoul, South Korea. He went on to earn an individual silver medal in the 100-meter backstroke and a team gold medal in the 4x100 medley relay, plus two more medals at the 1992 Olympics in Barcelona.[9]

Every backstroke record holder for the past two decades has used the so-called Berkoff Blastoff at the start of each race and the turn of each lap. Freestyle and butterfly winners have adopted it, too—including, most notably, Michael Phelps, who has broken thirty-seven world records in swimming over the years, and who won eight gold medals in the 2008 Olympics in Beijing.

So constantly ask yourself about perfection: "Who (or what) does this best in all the world, and how could I adapt their practices to my circumstances? For what subset of users can my product or service be an absolutely perfect solution? How would I do this if I weren't constrained by . . . ?"

Sometimes the issue isn't perfect performance, but perfect information—or the lack of it. For example, a product is often designed a particular way because its designer doesn't know something about the customer, how the customer will use the product, or how the distributor will handle it. But maybe the designer *could* know more, at least about a subset of customers and their uses of the product. If so, how could the design be enhanced?

Imagine perfection, and ask yourself:

How would we do things differently if we had perfect information about our customers and their usage habits, our distribution, and so on? In the vending machine business, there's a trade-off between effectiveness and efficiency. On one hand, of course, if a machine sits empty, the owner loses sales opportunities. On the other hand, to be efficient, a driver should restock a vending machine only when it's completely empty; nothing will eat up profits faster than having a driver take the time to constantly visit machines that don't really need refilling. So when should the driver plan to come by? Historically, the answer was based on averages—for example, on average, a Coke machine in a college dorm might need refilling every two days, but one in a public library might need refilling only once a week.

Now imagine perfection. In this context, perfect information would involve having the machine tell the vendor when it needs refilling. In fact, *truly* perfect information would involve having the machine tell the vendor not only when it needs refilling, but when it first ran out of the most popular items *and* how many times customers have requested those popular items since the machine ran out. That way, the vendor could decide whether to devote extra slots to the most popular items and reduce the space devoted to those items that customer settled on only because the most popular ones were not available. (He could even use the information to raise the price of the most popular items.) The idea? Build cell phone–like capability into the vending machines, so they can automatically "call" the vendor on a regular basis and report their status, item by item.[10]

What would we do differently if we could trust our customers not to cheat us (or didn't care that only a few did)? If you pause to think about it, a significant portion of the cost of many products is driven by the seller's efforts to prevent fraud or theft. Think about those credit checks you have to endure when you buy a car, or those long forms you have to fill out to file an insurance claim. In a world of product scanners, much of the value added by the checkout clerks in many stores is nothing more than preventing customers from stealing stuff.

Now consider how much money you, as a seller, might save if you could completely trust your customers, and whether there's an identifiable subset of customers or potential customers whom you know you can trust. After all, honor box candies—the ones in small offices where there's an open box of candy bars and you are simply "on your honor" to pay for them—have succeeded for decades.

Think this one works only in small-scale or low-value situations? Think again. USAA has been one of America's top-performing insurance companies for decades, in terms of both high service levels and low premiums, because it initially focused on a customer base that proved to be more trustworthy than average: military officers and their families.[11]

Want an interesting variation of this one? Self-checkout lanes in supermarkets (and, increasingly, other forms of retail stores) lower the labor cost of the checkout operation by 75 percent or more—which is more than enough to offset the occasional theft in the large majority of such stores.[12]

DISCOVERING UNRECOGNIZED "HEADROOM"

All of us—individuals, teams, companies, institutions, and even whole industries—conduct our work by employing a set of standard operating procedures (SOPs). This is perfectly reasonable; after all, who wants to rethink a task every time we do it?

SOPs might consist of "rules" in the formal sense—such as laws or government regulations—or they might simply consist of conventional wisdom or habits we've voluntarily adopted. In either case, they tend to take on a life of their own after a while. People become very reluctant to change them. But the world isn't made up of entirely identical situations, so the ideal operating procedure for a particular situation may not be the standard operating procedure at all. In addition, of course, the world changes all the time. And that change—especially if it's of the "many tiny changes" variety—often creates unnoticed cases in which even the new "average" situation no longer fits with the old SOPs.

Such situations create what we call "unrecognized headroom," where there's a significant opportunity to redefine or re-tailor a product or process to better fit the specific circumstances of the new situation—thereby providing headroom for performance to pop up above what was previously expected.

The first type of unrecognized headroom can be found by asking questions such as:

Where do the "rules" already provide more flexibility than we (or others) currently take advantage of? In the inimitable words of rock supergroup the Eagles, "So often times it happens that we live our lives in chains, and we never even know we have the key."

In mid-2007, Steve Humphries, a mortgage broker, and Kurt Bryan, an insurance salesman, were trying to solve an age-old problem.[13] Not a business problem, mind you—a *football* problem. You see, the two businessmen also served their community as football coaches at Piedmont High School near Oakland, California, and they were searching for ways to help their team compete more successfully against the other eighteen schools in East Bay Region 2A—seventeen of which had larger enrollments than Piedmont's.[14] The school's players were tired of being outmanned every Friday night, and Messrs. Humphries and Bryan were searching relentlessly for ways to help their young Davids slay more Goliaths.

A year earlier, while discussing the merits of "trick plays"—misdirection plays traditionally employed only on very rare occasions to help one team catch the opposing team off guard and thereby neutralize its superior strength or speed—they had hit upon a powerful Right Question when Humphries asked Bryan: "What if we had an *entire offense* of trick plays?" Fascinated by this notion, the pair had spent more than twelve months scouring the California high school federation rule book looking for legal means of confusing the defensive behemoths their players regularly faced—until at last Bryan noticed something in the "scrimmage kick formation" rule.[15]

Here's how ESPN.com later explained it: "Normally used for punts, the rule stated that as long as the player receiving the snap was seven yards deep behind the center, any teammate wearing the jersey of an eligible receiver (between numbers 1 and 49 or 80 and 89) was permitted to go downfield. [This meant] Bryan and Humphries . . . could potentially send *any* of their 11 players out for passes."[16]

That fall, Piedmont High debuted the Piedmont A–11 (for "all 11 players eligible") Offense, filled with alien formations, constant presnap shifts, and unconventional plays—and piloted by an undersized 150-pound quarterback. Bedlam ensued. "According to *Scientific American*, the typical offensive formation has 36 post-snap scenarios of who can take the ball from under center and where it can go. Bryan and Humphries [had] discovered a way to increase the permutations to an eye-popping 16,632."[17]

After losing the first two games of the 2007 season as players learned the new system, Piedmont High ran off seven straight victories and qualified for the state playoffs. Then they qualified again in 2008. And again in 2009—even after subsequent rule changes placed certain limits on their formerly unlimited options. Meanwhile, hundreds of other high schools have adopted the Piedmont A–11 Offense, leveling the playing field for smaller schools all over the nation. All because of a single Right Question—and coaches Bryan and Humphries's willingness to look long and hard for valuable flexibility within a current set of rules.

"Where are we operating under a set of 'rules' that we've accepted for a long time without ever going back and reexamining what the current rules actually say?" For example, we were once part of a team that helped a telecommunications company improve its call centers. Many of the call center managers had been with the company for years, and had grown up in an atmosphere of highly restrictive work rules. When the team leader insisted that the call center managers actually go back and study the latest union contract, the managers found—much to their surprise—that many of the restrictive work rules that had been in place when the center was established, and which they had internalized as everlasting SOPs, were long gone. Suddenly, all kinds of new ideas sprang forth.

The second type of unrecognized headroom can be found by understanding that companies and industries usually take time to fully incorporate the effects of new technologies or regulatory changes into their behavior. A long time. In fact, it's been estimated that society takes about forty years to fully capitalize on major new technologies. Given the rate of technological and regulatory change in the world today, this delay creates opportunities everywhere. To make sure you spot them, ask yourself questions like this:

Which technologies underlying our production and operating processes have changed the most since we last redesigned our product or last rebuilt our manufacturing and distribution systems? For example, how can life insurance and health insurance companies take advantage of the findings we seem to read about every day regarding genetic markers for hereditary diseases? Why don't home appliance manufacturers build into their refrigerators, air conditioners, washers, and dryers the same predictors of failure and cell phone capabilities that the jet engine manufacturers and vending machine makers of the world did in the examples we mentioned earlier?

Once you've built a strong starter list of Right Questions by looking at others who came up with a great idea when faced with the challenge you face, add your own best insights from your own past challenges to your list. After all, you've been creative before, too. Think back: when you've had your own biggest breakthroughs in the past, what questions did you ask—or could you have asked—to generate those breakthroughs? (Just be careful, as noted earlier, to eliminate any questions you *always* seem to ask; they're probably worn out by now.)

Next, add to your list of Right Questions over time by watching the world around you. Every time you see a great idea—one that makes you say "Wow!," or "I wish I had thought of that"—take note of the idea and try to come up with the question that would have guided you to it. Then try to come up with at least four other answers to the question—because remember, great questions have many possible answers.

One final thought as you develop your arsenal. Don't get trapped by overfocusing on *today's* ideation problem. Many well-intentioned people get caught without a relevant arsenal of questions because the arsenal they've built contains questions that pertain only to challenges they've already planned for, not the ones they're now called upon to undertake.

Think broadly about your likely future needs. What are *all* the types of ideas you may be called on to develop in the next year or two? Today your task may be to improve a product, but next month you may be called upon to improve service levels. Start now to collect questions across the full spectrum, because some types of questions are easier to collect than others—and because you don't want to be caught short of Right Questions when the need for a great idea arises suddenly and unexpectedly, as it does in our next chapter.

3

When It's Time to Find a Better Idea

So when it comes time to think of an idea, you simply pull out a couple of questions, maybe grab some colleagues, and go at it, right? Well, actually, you *could* do exactly that, and you might even surprise yourself at how effective you'd be. But with some care, you and your fellow thinkers can be even more effective.

Once you've developed an arsenal of questions, you need to choose the right ones to address your current challenge. What's more, you need to tailor them to the specific situation you're in and, in most cases, provide one or more signpost examples to ensure that you get the most from your designated problem solver(s), whether that means you alone or an entire team of people.

CHOOSING THE RIGHT QUESTIONS FROM YOUR ARSENAL

If your experience proves to be anything like ours, you'll be able to build a formidable list of good questions in virtually no time. We built a list of over 100 truly powerful questions for new business and product ideas in under six weeks—and of course we didn't have the luxury of a starter list like the one in Chapter 2 or the appendix at the end of this book!

But which questions should you choose from your list when you're suddenly and unexpectedly called upon? You may only have the time to work with a small subset of your list. In later chapters, we'll discuss in more detail how many questions to use, but for now, let's just say that the number can vary from as few as three to as many as thirty or more, depending on whether you're working alone or with a group of people. However many you choose, the principles for which ones to choose are the same: you want to ensure that each *individual* question is productive, and that the *collection* of questions combine to create a productive portfolio.

All the questions in your arsenal are good, so don't worry about comparing their intrinsic quality. Instead, focus on achieving a tight fit between the questions and the specific task you face. First each question must pass four tests individually.

Does the question either target an aspect of the problem that has received little attention in the past or force a significantly different perspective than has been taken in the past? In chapter 1, we told you it was okay to use a question that others have used before—and it is. You can find lots of great ideas by reusing someone else's question. But your odds of finding a truly breakthrough idea are higher if you use a question that gives you a truly unique view of the situation.

Let's look again at our three heroes from Compaq. They were not the only entrepreneurs looking to make a fortune in the personal computer space at that time—the market was being flooded with so-called PC clones. But the other PC clones concentrated primarily on bringing down costs (and therefore prices). The genius of Compaq's founders was to look for an improvement that was fundamentally different in nature from what others were looking for—an improvement that would matter greatly to a significant segment of the market.

Can't think of an aspect or perspective that hasn't already been investigated by others? Try looking at an existing area, but then dramatically ramp up the standard of success. Consider the idea that led

Dell Computer to land on the list of Z–1–4 companies. As the above paragraph makes clear, Dell wasn't the first of the PC clone makers to ask the question "How can we reduce costs (and therefore prices)?" But Dell's cost (and price) reduction aspirations went far beyond the five to ten percent solutions sought by others. Dell wanted to achieve a truly radical improvement in cost—and that higher level of aspiration forced a new perspective ("We can't possibly achieve *that* level of cost reduction unless we . . .").

Dell succeeded spectacularly. It found a way to reduce prices by about 40 percent relative to comparable machines.[1] One key to success? Eliminating the retailer. In the early and mid-1980s, personal computers were a relatively new invention. Customers needed education about what "RAM" meant, what "buss bars" were, what a computer's hard disk capacity implied about its ability to run certain programs, and so on. That education was typically supplied by the retailers—in fact, a single sale often involved several hours of a salesperson's time. As a result, the retailers—understandably—marked up the prices of computers substantially.

Dell recognized that a small but growing portion of computer buyers had developed sufficient technical knowledge that they didn't need such hand-holding. Dell opted to sell directly over the phone, eliminating the retailer and those customers it didn't want to serve, the ones who would take up too much time asking lots of novice-level questions.

More recently, there's been an equally powerful revolution in the automobile industry. Automakers are always looking for ways to control the cost of their cars. But in 2003, Ratan Tata, chairman of India's largest conglomerate, the Tata Group, adopted an unusually aggressive, ramping-up-the-standard-of-success perspective to the issue. He envisioned a "people's car" for India, a modern car that would be affordable within the budgets of India's emerging middle class. Thus, he set the target price of the car at 100,000 Indian rupees, or about U.S. $2,171. That's right—a brand-new car that would sell for about $2,000, around half the price of the next cheapest competitor.

How did his team go about fulfilling his vision? They and their suppliers asked questions—lots of them. As one of the company's suppliers put it, "It's basically throwing out everything the auto industry had thought about cost structures, taking out a clean sheet of paper and asking, 'What's possible?'" After interviewing Tata's engineers, one newspaper described the project by saying, "their guiding philosophy was 'Do we really need that?'"[2]

The Tata Nano, a rear-engine four-passenger city car, launched commercially on March 23, 2009.[3] The basic model has no heating or air conditioning, only one side mirror, and only three lug nuts per wheel instead of the more traditional four or five. The trunk is accessed only from the rear seat.

But it's safe, passing all government safety standards. And efficient, going as far as 52 miles per gallon in the city and 61 miles per gallon on the highway.[4] And, incredibly, it did indeed go on sale for 100,000 rupees, or U.S. $2,171.[5] To give you an idea of that achievement, Henry Ford's Model T—the first American car built for the masses, which debuted exactly 100 years before the Nano—was introduced at a price that was the equivalent of $20,091 in today's dollars, or nine times higher than the price of Mr. Tata's automotive achievement.

And has the Nano been successful in the marketplace? Well, Tata booked over 200,000 orders for it, generating revenues of $434 million, in the first two weeks after its introduction. [6]

Does the question itself suggest directions that fit your specific current needs? For example, pretend you're conducting a short-term cost reduction program. You need ideas that can be implemented quickly and cheaply, and that pay off in a short period of time. You'd be right on the money to ask such questions as "What circumstances cause us to deviate from whatever are the most efficient ways of handling each step in our business process?" Such a question could help you identify problems where customers ask for (but then aren't willing to pay for) special designs or special administrative procedures. It could help you identify where rework occurs because the field sales force submits incorrect or incomplete orders.

On the other hand, asking "Where have the technical requirements of certain jobs changed, such that current personnel are experiencing difficulty meeting the new standard?" would likely be less productive. Even though the payoff from the second question might ultimately be larger than from the first, any solutions suggested by the second question would likely require personnel replacements or training, both of which could be time consuming and expensive—and if you're conducting a short-term cost reduction program, that doesn't fit with your specific current needs.

Is there information available that will actually answer the question? Nothing slows down the flow of ideas like a great question to which the truthful answer is "There's no way to ever find out." Don't laugh; it's happened to us, more often than we like to admit. But be careful—there's a major difference between "we don't know the answer *right now*" and "there's no way to *ever* know the answer."

Obviously, if there's information available at your fingertips to answer the question, you're in great shape. Equally obviously, if there's no way to ever answer it, move on to another question. But not so obviously, if you hear "We don't know the answer right now," don't be too quick to give up on your question. In fact, as we'll discuss in more detail in Chapter 5, you may well end up preferring a question where the information is *not* at your fingertips—because that may well mean that no one else has figured out yet that the information is actually quite valuable.

Does the question prompt ideas that the implementing organization will embrace— or ones that require major changes in the status quo? If you depend on an existing organization to implement your new ideas, you shouldn't waste your time with questions designed to produce completely radical answers. In fact, one of our own great failures occurred for this very reason.

We served a large service company that had grown from a start-up to rank third in its industry. The CEO and board asked us to find a way for the company to move into the number two position. And we did—in fact, we struck the mother lode.

In this industry, individual stores could make a profit even if they produced less than 50 percent of the sales volume they were staffed to handle. (Surprised? It happens all the time. Think about barbershops. If they just could keep all the barbers busy throughout the day, they'd make a killing. The same holds true for dry cleaners, restaurants, tool rental stores, and so on.) If you moved a store's utilization factor from its current 50 percent to 75 percent, its profits would double.

Further, the central factories that each company in the industry used to supply its stores were also busy less than 50 percent of the time. And, in a final quirk, the number two player in the industry had made some strategic and operating mistakes in recent years, so its stock price was very low.

Once we took a slightly different perspective on the situation than the one our client had been taking, we hit on an idea that was as powerful as it was (suddenly) obvious: our client, the number three player, should acquire its larger rival! We had never seen such synergies. The newly combined company would immediately be the industry's largest. The excess costs that could be removed just by combining two sets of factories into one set, and closing the others, could more than justify the deal. On top of that, finding ways to combine even a fraction of the two companies' sets of stores (which could potentially be done without customers even noticing) could double the newly combined company's profits *again*. And there were more synergies beyond even those.

We were elated—and naïve. Our client *hated* the other company. In fact, he had founded his own company based on the disrespect he had for the number two player—a disrespect that had grown into outright disdain over the twenty-plus years that followed. Although he could rationally recognize all the benefits of the acquisition, the thought of being associated with that other company literally made him unable to sleep at night. The idea went nowhere.

Learn from our blunder. Some questions point to changes your organization can embrace, while others may point to directions that, while potentially feasible in another organization, simply won't fly within yours. Said another way, Tiffany and Cartier aren't going to sell plastic jewelry on QVC, no matter how large the opportunity appears to be.

Once you have a list of questions that are individually productive, it's time to examine them as a portfolio. Your goal is to develop a collection of questions that will strike the right balance between covering as many new perspectives as is practical and covering each perspective in enough depth to tap its full potential.

It's a judgment call, of course, and the right balance varies with the number of separate ideation sessions that will be involved in your search for a new idea. (For our purposes, an "ideation session" is defined as an event in which you or a small group of three to five people focus all your attention on one single Right Question for a concentrated period of thirty to forty-five minutes.) Let's take two extremes: three ideation sessions versus thirty.

If you'll be having only three ideation sessions, you'll likely want the questions to be radically different from each other, in order to force very different perspectives on the problem. You'll want questions for which you can identify multiple, widely different signpost example ideas to illustrate the range of ideas you wish to invent, to ensure that each of your three questions is explored broadly.

On the other hand, if you'll be using thirty questions, you may prefer using a number of somewhat more similar questions to force the exploration of useful new perspectives in less breadth but greater depth. For example, imagine you worked at Ford back in 1940 and you were looking to invent a new type of car. Not new types of ships, trains, or airplanes—just cars. Instead of asking radically different questions, you might have chosen to ask several nearly identical questions that explored subtle differences in the standard design of cars. Asking, "*For whom* is today's standard car design least well suited?" might have led you to think about large families and invent the station wagon, or perhaps about single persons and invent an early precursor of today's smart car. But phrasing the question only slightly differently and asking, "For *what occasions* is today's standard car design least well suited?" might have led you to see completely different opportunities such as sports cars or Range Rovers.

TAILORING QUESTIONS AND USING SIGNPOST EXAMPLES

Many people ask us why, in the car example you just read, we had to ask both the "for whom?" and "for what occasions?" versions of the same question. You, too, might think that either phrasing of the question should lead a bright, creative thinker to come up with both sets of ideas. And you'd be right—occasionally. However, our experience applying Brainsteering in hundreds of situations has taught us that most people, even highly creative ones, think better if you tailor the question in one of several ways and provide signpost examples to illustrate the kind of answers you're looking for.

Tailoring is required because, surprisingly, most people can't effectively translate a general question to a specific situation if that situation is different from the general situation in any material way. We first learned this when we received reports of an early Brainsteering workshop run by one of our colleagues that had been judged a complete failure. Failure? We had seen some Brainsteering workshops go better than others, but a complete failure?! As you would imagine, we raced to learn what went wrong.

The client was an automotive parts manufacturer. The purpose of the overall project was to determine whether the client could use its capabilities to make parts for lawn mowers, and the purpose of that particular workshop was to look for entry opportunities. So our colleague and the client team had employed questions such as "For which users is our product least well suited?"; "What's the biggest hassle about using our product?"; and so on. The attendees dutifully answered the questions—*about automobiles.* Not surprisingly, they found little of relevance for the lawn mower business.

Apparently, it never occurred to our colleague, nor to any member of the client team, that the words "our product" should be changed to "the current products in the lawn mower marketplace." As a result, twenty people sat through a day of torturous ideation sessions, wondering how this workshop was supposed to be helpful but never asking "What if I apply this general question to the specific problem we're trying to solve?"

Unfortunately, that's not the only time we've seen a too-general question cause thinkers to fall short of their goals. In one case where our question was not tailored specifically enough, a participant told us, "I didn't realize that 'the biggest hassle of using our product' could include hassles associated with *disposing* of it"—hassles that were quite significant in that product category. In another case, one person interpreted the usually productive question "For whom is our product least well suited?" to mean that he should list all the customers whose needs weren't met by his company's current product—but not even attempt to describe how or why the product failed to meet their needs, or to draw implications about potential changes to the product—even though the stated goal of the workshop was "to identify potential product improvements."

The moral of the story? Ask yourself how narrowly or literally you and/or your colleagues tend to interpret questions, and tailor your questions accordingly. Some people have trouble dealing with abstract concepts, while others may be insulted if your questions get too specific.

Another helpful device that requires you to make some judgment calls when working with other people to develop ideas is the use of signpost examples. Up to this point in the book, we've tried to provide you with signpost examples to illustrate various kinds of successful answers to each of the most important questions we've introduced. Remember when we prepared to send you off to answer the "emotionally powerful as a child/expensive form for adults" question? We provided you with over a dozen signpost examples ranging from gourmet jelly beans to space tourism. This not only increased your confidence, it also gave you some specific dimensions along which you could expand your thinking.

Signpost examples can be very helpful. But whether you should or shouldn't use them depends on your question and your audience. If the precise meaning of your question is clearly obvious to your particular audience, then you don't need to use signpost examples. If the meaning is less obvious for any reason, an example or two can be very helpful.

Just be careful, because there's a trade-off: the more specifically you guide a group of thinkers with signpost examples, the greater will be their tendency to fill in the blanks, simply parroting back variants of the examples you gave them. There are times when that may be just what you want from a particular group, but usually it's not. That's why, when we're leading client workshops, we're judicious about the number of questions for which we provide signpost examples. When we do provide them (which we do most of the time), we try to provide only one or two, and we try to make them illustrate very different possibilities within the conceptual space covered by the question.

That's almost it for Part I. If you put the book down now and never pick it up again, you'll already be a stronger source of new ideas. For many of you, that may be enough. But if you want to be truly great, read on.

In fact, as an incentive to keep reading, we'd like to end Part I with something special. Something that could help you solve one of your biggest personal ideation challenges. You know, the one that every adult in America faces several times a year—and usually fails. We are, of course, referring to finding the perfect gift for your favorite hard-to-buy-for loved one or friend.

FINDING THE PERFECT GIFT

It's hard enough to find the perfect gift for people you don't know very well—but it's usually even harder to find one for loved ones or close friends. Why? Because the closer you are to them, the more likely you are to have exhausted your reservoir of ideas. Let's say you've been married for ten years. If you've given your wife or husband just one gift each year for her or his birthday, for Christmas/Chanukah, for Valentine's Day, and for your wedding anniversary, you're about to go hunting for their forty-first gift. And if you've typically given them more than one, or if you've also given them gifts for Mother's Day or Father's Day, you could be looking for their fifty-first or sixty-first gift. No wonder you're out of good ideas!

Can you use Brainsteering to help you find that perfect gift—the one that's truly original and thoughtful, that's sure to be one they'll like, that catches them by surprise, and that's unique to you? One that makes your loved one ask admiringly, "How did you *ever* think of this?" Of course you can—simply by doing exactly what Brainsteering always does: asking yourself questions that force you to look at things from perspectives you don't normally take.

Let's run a miniature one-person Brainsteering workshop on this topic. All you'll need is a pen, a pad of paper, and thirty minutes. Ready?

Start by picking whatever you consider to be the best three questions from the list below. The questions are associated with three categories of gifts, which vary in appropriateness based on your relationship with your intended gift recipient: "heart-warming," "hobbies and interests," and "giver-centric."

For each question, read both the question and the signpost

explanation that goes with it. Then spend ten minutes working with that question—and that question *only*—jotting down the ideas that come to you. Don't stop to evaluate them, just write.

If you're like most people, you'll generate between two and four ideas in response to each of the three questions you choose. It won't feel like you're making much progress (after all, two to four ideas in ten minutes feels very slow at the time). But that's okay—after ten minutes, just go on to the next question and repeat the process.

After thirty minutes, you'll have a list of about six to twelve ideas—and the odds are that you'll really like one or two of them. More important, your intended recipient will like them too—at least a lot more than that sweater you were planning to give them.

HEARTWARMING GIFTS

What was their favorite toy, hobby, or activity during the period of their life on which they look back most fondly?

Can you obtain the toy? For example, we found a mint-condition 1968 toy Batmobile on eBay for someone who had been a huge fan of ABC's *Batman* TV series as a child. He still keeps it on his desk at work, and smiles every time he looks at it. We also know someone who includes among his all-time favorite gifts a stuffed snowman named Mr. Bingle—because receiving a Mr. Bingle for Christmas when he was three years old is the earliest memory he has of his childhood.

Can you give them an enhanced version of whatever they cherished? A woman we know desperately wanted a Pound Puppy stuffed animal one Christmas when she was a child, but didn't get it. Recently, her boyfriend overjoyed her—not just by giving her a Pound Puppy, but by giving her an entire collection of eighty Pound Puppies.

Can you find a way for them to relive a cherished experience—together with you? Our father is a lifelong Civil War buff. As a child, he studied every battle, every campaign. We put together a weekend car tour tracing General Sherman's Atlanta campaign, stopping at each of the major battlefields and tracing both the conduct of each battle and how it led to the next. All the information was available for free on the Internet; it was simply a matter of taking the time to collect it in one place, print it, and bind it at Kinko's. We had a blast.

What event or accomplishment in their life are they most proud of?
Do you know? If so, what memento of that occasion can you get for her? If not, then maybe your gift is simply asking her out to dinner for the explicit purpose—which you'll tell her in advance—of having her tell you the full story of that memorable event or accomplishment.

What place, person, or group of people were they once very fond of, but have since lost touch with?
How can he revisit that place, either physically or in spirit? The most obvious way is by taking a trip, but there are also less obvious (and less expensive) ways to accomplish the same thing. The Internet is a great place to find pictures of almost anything these days. Or there's often a small-town newspaper whose photographer is both underutilized and underpaid, and who would probably be delighted to go photograph your intended recipient's old house, or high school, or whatever.

How can you help her reconnect with that person or group of people? A friend of ours recently contacted a long list of his wife's best friends from several different phases of her life, and asked each of them to send him some memento of their happiest times together—a photo, a song, a homemade video, anything. He compiled them into a sixty-minute video presentation—and blew her away when he gave it to her for her fiftieth birthday.

HOBBIES AND INTERESTS GIFTS

What would be the ultimate experience associated with his hobby or interest, and how could he have that experience (or a proxy for it)?

Who are/were the ultimate players and/or the ultimate moments associated with his hobby? Let's say he's a sports fan—can you arrange for him to meet one of his idols, or to meet someone who once played with him or her and could relate fascinating stories? Would memorabilia associated with his idols—trading cards, a uniform (original or replica), and so on—mean a lot to him? Many people find autographs to be incredibly meaningful; the most emotionally uplifting gift we ever gave to one particular teen was an autographed picture of her favorite movie star, Leonardo DiCaprio.

What equipment is associated with his hobby? Is there a piece of equipment associated with his hobby that is exactly what his idol used or would use, even if it's outlandishly beyond what he actually needs at his level of proficiency? He probably doesn't play golf quite as well as Tiger Woods does, and you may not be able to afford the clubs Tiger uses—but you could buy him exactly the same club head covers or golf glove or rain slicker that Tiger uses. (Notice that we didn't suggest buying the same golf balls, golf shirt, or golf hat—after all, you're shooting for the unique, not the obvious.)

Is there a new invention that dramatically changes how well she can perform an important aspect of her hobby, or even her daily routine?

We're not talking about just buying her the latest kitchen gadget—you've already played that card in the past. To be a great gift, this one has to represent a dramatic change in her experience. For example, a couple of years ago, one of our spouses bought her mother in Eastern Europe a laptop computer. On the surface, that hardly seems like a breakthrough gift—but the daughter had programmed it with a software product that had been introduced only two years before: Skype video-telephony, a service that enables the user to make free video calls almost anywhere in the world. Her mother still knows very little about that English-language-based computer—but she knows which five buttons to push to let her see her baby grandchild "live and in color" on her computer screen every single day.

GIVER-CENTRIC GIFTS

What pleasant secret or experience do only the two of you share?
A gift from you becomes special if it emphasizes the connection between you. For example, another friend of ours and his spouse have a pet phrase they use to express their affection for each other, summed up in an acronym whose meaning is known only to them. Every once in a while, she discovers that phrase hidden in gifts, such as a necklace he once gave her for their anniversary, in which the beautiful glass beads that seemed to be arranged in random order actually spelled out their secret acronym in Morse code.

Similarly, the two of us shared a childhood experience that involved a favorite toy called the Anzio Invader being accidentally run over by our father as he backed his car out of the garage. To this day, there remains a running joke between us as to who was at fault for leaving the toy in the driveway—and for years, each of us has searched for an original Anzio Invader with which to repay the other one.

What is the perfect gift that only he could give you—and what does that tell you about the perfect gift that you could give him?
This one's easy—and as the saying goes, turnabout is fair play.

What do you do better than most people, but have never used to create a gift before?
This one can be terrific, but only if you have never done it before. We know of a man who'd been quite a singer as a child—but neither his wife nor his children had ever heard him sing, because he hadn't performed in public since high school. He secretly took singing lessons for six months, then

conspired with a friend's son, who had an amateur recording studio set up in his basement. One karaoke tape and a few hours later, he had the year's big hit at his family's Christmas gift exchange.

As always, now that you've seen the process demonstrated, you can use the other Brainsteering techniques to expand your own list. For example, ask yourself, "What are the gifts that I've seen make the biggest emotional impact on the recipient, and what was the question that could have led the giver to think of them?" You know the rest.

So, did you succeed? If so, congratulations! Let's review what you applied here, so you can apply it in other situations.

You used a series of powerful questions. Each question met the various criteria we established in chapter 2 and earlier in this chapter.

You used the signpost examples we provided to help you to explore several different meanings of the same question.

You focused on answering each question for long enough to get past your first (usually mediocre) idea. In fact, if you're like most people, you returned during the last few minutes of at least one of your ten-minute mini ideation sessions to an idea that had intrigued you earlier but initially exhibited some problem or barrier. By returning to that idea, instead of abandoning it and skipping ahead to a different question, you found a better variant of the idea, or a way around the key problem or barrier, or another change that made the idea work.

By the end, you may have thought of one or more new questions that were even better than the ones we asked. If so, we'll console ourselves by claiming that you might not have thought of them had you not gone through our starter set first. . . .

PART II

TAKE YOUR PERSONAL IDEATION
SKILLS TO THE MAX

4

A Systematic Approach to Developing Questions

Don't you hate it when you realize you've had a blind spot? When you suddenly think to yourself, "Damn, I should have thought of that—the answer was right in front of my face!" Even the most creative people experience this feeling all the time. It happens because people's minds often fall into ruts. In attacking a challenge, we usually follow the same patterns of thought that helped us succeed last time.

The best way to avoid falling into a mental rut is to develop a systematic approach to your search, an approach that will ensure you've been comprehensive in developing the Right Questions to ask.

A couple of years ago, we worked with a successful fashion magazine. The magazine was innovative. It was a market leader. And it was highly profitable (which, as anyone in the publishing field will tell you, is rare these days). But in looking for story angles each week, they had always identified ideas using only their intuition—they had never stepped back, looked at the big picture, and used a systematic approach. When we showed them such an approach as part of their introduction to Brainsteering, it took the editor in chief only a few minutes to burst forth with a sudden realization: "We've never written a single story on the demise of a fashion! We only cover what's new, not what our readers should *stop* wearing!" A whole new avenue of potential future articles opened up in that instant.

If you want to avoid blind spots; if you need not just a few questions but *many* questions; if you need the *best* questions; or if you need to be sure that you've considered *all* the possibilities—then you need a methodical, comprehensive approach. In any of these circumstances, you need to employ a systematic approach that will enable you to scan the entire universe of potential questions, rather than simply selecting a few of your favorite questions from a list you've compiled from past experience. In this chapter, we'll teach you just such an approach.

And by the way, the same approach can be applied when it comes time to *answer* a question—again, if you need many ideas, or the best idea, or to consider all the possibilities.

But be warned: a systematic approach to developing questions requires patience and perseverance. As you search every possible nook and cranny of an issue for good ideas, you'll have to explore even the lower probability or lower payoff portions of the issue, not just the easier, more obvious higher probability or higher payoff portions. For many problems, a fully comprehensive approach could actually be overkill—after all, in some cases, you need just one or two great ideas.

Sometimes it's best to combine an intuitive approach with a more systematic approach in your search for the right questions. In our work with clients, we'll sometimes work in random patterns for part of our search, jumping from question to question, while at other times in that very same search, we'll sweep the landscape of possibilities quite thoroughly.

THE CONCEPT OF "MECE"

At the heart of every systematic approach (to anything, not just formulating questions) lies a deceptively simple concept: MECE (pronounced MEE-see), which stands for "mutually exclusive [and] collectively exhaustive." MECE describes any way of subdividing a collection of items so that every item in that collection appears in one, and only one, part. In layperson's terms, think of it as meaning that your categorization scheme has "no overlaps [mutually exclusive] and no gaps [collectively exhaustive]."

Perhaps the quickest way to fully appreciate MECE is to visualize it. Imagine a flat game board. If we asked you to divide up all the space on that game board, there are a million ways you could do it. Let's look at two groups of ways.

In the first group, you could draw horizontal lines, vertical lines, or both, on the board, and the subsections enclosed by your lines could be your categorization scheme. The lines could be straight, as on a checkerboard, or curvy, as in a jigsaw puzzle, but either way you would create a MECE scheme—that is, you could divide up the game board into a discrete set of subsections with "no overlaps [mutually exclusive] and no gaps [collectively exhaustive]."

Both of these gameboard designs are MECE—that is, they have no overlaps and no gaps

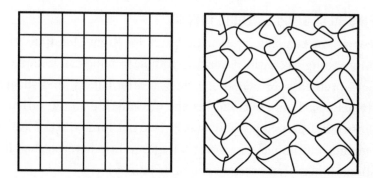

Figure 4.1: MECE Schemes For Dividing A Gameboard

In the second group, you could draw several circles on the board, then declare that your scheme includes "all the areas within the circles." Your scheme could have circles that overlap, and there could be gaps between the circles—but in either case, you'd have a *non*-MECE scheme.

This gameboard design is *non*-MECE, as the areas within the circles overlap, and there are gaps

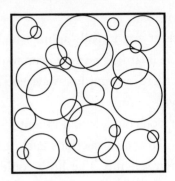

Figure 4.2: Non-MECE Scheme For Dividing A Gameboard

Having a MECE scheme when searching for questions is extremely useful, because it improves our ability to be both effective (by being exhaustive) and efficient (by ensuring that we look at each possibility only once).

KEEPING MECE SIMPLE: "LOGIC TREES"

Whenever you conduct a systematic search for Right Questions, there's one more thing to consider: keeping your search logically simple.

Let's pretend your neighbor owned a little bakery, and she asked you to help her figure out whether she was offering all the varieties of muffins that she could possibly make given her limited set of available ingredients, muffin pans, and ovens. Eager to help her, you start firing questions at her: "Let's see, do you offer . . .

small, warm blackberry sugar-free muffins?"
large, warm blueberry sugar muffins?"
large, hot blueberry sugar muffins?"
large, hot blackberry sugar muffins?"
small, warm blueberry sugar muffins?"

large, warm blackberry sugar muffins?"
large, warm blueberry sugar-free muffins?"
small, hot blackberry sugar muffins?"
large, hot blackberry sugar-free muffins?"
small, hot blueberry sugar-free muffins?"
small, hot blackberry sugar-free muffins?"
large, warm blackberry sugar-free muffins?"
small, hot blueberry sugar muffins?"
small, warm blueberry sugar-free muffins?"
large, hot blueberry sugar-free muffins?"

If she answered "yes" to each question, you could quickly declare, "Yep—you offer every variety of muffin that you could possibly make given your constraints." But would you be right?

Before you answer, ask yourself, "Are my questions actually MECE?" There are so many factors being considered simultaneously that it's nearly impossible to tell whether all the combinations have actually been covered or not. Further, the various types of muffins are listed in a random sequence, making it harder to keep track of which varieties you've already asked about.

Any search technique that introduces sudden complexity actually impedes your ability to be MECE. As this example illustrates, it's difficult to simply whip together a MECE list of questions for a situation that involves any significant degree of complexity—how do you know whether you've left out an important one? Therefore, we need a technique that starts out simple, then adds complexity only slowly, and maintains the MECE standard at every step so that nothing gets lost along the way.

The best technique for meeting these requirements is the logic tree. A logic tree starts with a universal question. Then it subdivides that question into a small number of subquestions that are MECE. The smaller the number of subquestions, the easier it is to tell whether they are, in fact, MECE. Each resulting subquestion is then broken down into the next level of detail, and so on. Very soon, the branches of inquiry begin to resemble a tree that's been turned on its side. Here is just such a tree for our question about muffin varieties:

Did you consider *all* the possibilities, or did you miss one?

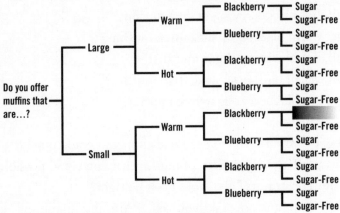

Figure 4.3: Logic Tree—Muffin Varieties

Notice that each branch divides into only two subbranches, even though (in this particular case) the types of branches are similar to others on the same level. Also notice how quickly you can spot a missing muffin type: small, warm blackberry sugar muffins.

A more sophisticated illustration of a logic tree's value in developing questions comes from some new product work we did a few years ago. Our client, a manufacturing company, spotted the market potential for a lower priced product, but it was critical that the product maintain the same functionality as current products in the marketplace. That is, the product itself could not be simplified or have any features removed just to reduce its cost. Instead, the client needed to find a way to reduce the actual manufacturing cost. Before diving in with random ideas, we decided to identify where the largest opportunities for improvements might be, so we built a logic tree of questions to break down cost differences according to their underlying causes. Here's the portion of the resulting logic tree that was related to materials cost (converted from manufacturing-speak into layperson's terms, of course):

How might a company drive its materials cost down below its key competitor?

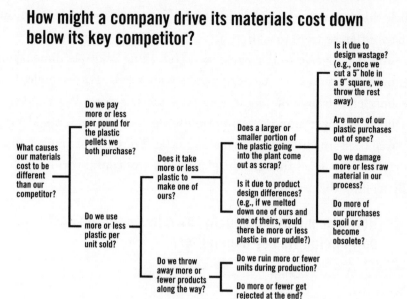

Figure 4.4: Logic Tree—Materials Cost Differences
Based On Consumption/Scrap Issues

With this cost breakdown in hand, we were able to focus our efforts on capturing the largest opportunities (which, in this particular case, were in product design differences and design wastage).

Note the construction of the tree. It starts with a single question, then breaks down that question into a small number of subquestions that are MECE. Then it breaks down those subquestions into more subquestions that are also MECE, and so on. (Importantly, the small number of branches at each level of the tree makes it easy to test whether the breakdown at that level is, in fact, MECE.) The result? The end questions of the tree are specific enough that they provide helpful guidance about where to search for cost improvements without being so detailed that the scope of any question would be overly narrow. Exactly the kind of things you want in a successful tree.

Interestingly, just as many Right Questions can lead you to a great idea, many different logic trees can lead you to a great idea. Just as there's no such thing as a "universal" Right Question, there's also no such thing as a "universal" logic tree—in fact, it's possible to create many different trees to address any one particular problem.

You may decide to disaggregate a tree along multiple dimensions before you hit on one that truly meets your needs. For example, let's reconsider the previous logic tree on materials cost. We happened to break it down along consumption/scrap lines. But we could have broken the same problem down along other lines, like manufacturing variances, if we had thought the plant had significant difficulties actually making the product.

How *else* might a company drive its materials cost down below its key competitor?

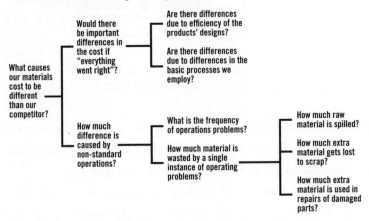

Figure 4.5: Alternate Logic Tree—Materials Cost Differences
Based On Manufacturing Variances

For still more alternatives, we might have created a tree broken down by product type, or by differences in the manufacturing processes employed, if we had thought more material was wasted when the products were made by hand versus by machine, and so on.

Just like selecting and tailoring Right Questions, or deciding when to use signpost examples, you have to use your judgment—in this case, to construct whatever type of logic tree best fits your particular situation, best leverages the best available data, and best illuminates the dimensions of your challenge in whatever ways you believe will prove most fruitful.

Based on what we just told you about using your judgment, you can well imagine that constructing logic trees is not all science—there's an art to it as well. Any two people will design the same tree differently. For that reason, constructing logic trees is best done alone. If you're working as part of a group, go away and design your tree, then present it to the group. Let them follow your logic and then agree or disagree, versus trying to develop it jointly. If more than one person wants to participate in the process of designing trees, that's terrific—but let each of them go away and design their trees separately, and then compare them. It's much easier to reconcile multiple trees, each of which has a logic flow that's internally consistent, than to have multiple thinkers advocating different, competing logic schemes at every branch of development.

CONSTRUCTING THE MOST USEFUL LOGIC TREES

Now that you understand the idea of a MECE logic tree, consider the following. Pretend that you want to generate significant new sales from an existing product. Pretend, too, that you need to look solely for product modifications that might be helpful. You could start with a very simple logic tree of questions.

How might a company build its business by modifying its existing product?

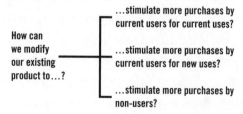

Figure 4.6: First-Level Logic Tree—Potential Product Improvements

Okay so far. But it's hard to generate Right Questions at that level of generality, so you decide to break each branch down further. A common mistake at this point is to try to be completely comprehensive and precise. That might include taking the bottom branch of the tree, "How can we modify our existing product to stimulate more purchases by nonusers?" and expanding it like this:

How might a company modify its existing product to attract new users?

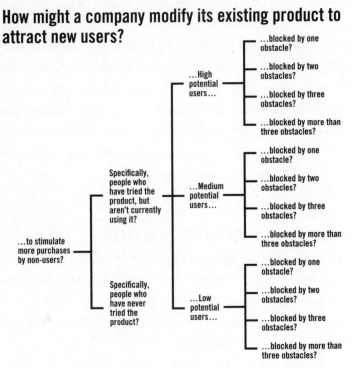

Figure 4.7: Second-Level Logic Tree—Potential Types Of New Users

Whoa! That last layer on the right could suddenly end up with a lot of questions and involve a lot of arbitrary divisions (especially if the middle layers were also broken into more divisions—for example, if potential users, instead of being divided into "high, medium, low," were divided into "first through fifth quintiles"). This tree could become so complicated that its tediousness would destroy the very creativity we're seeking to inspire, even if we did have the resolve to discuss every branch separately.

Clearly, to make logic trees more useful, a sanity check is warranted—and that sanity check consists of pruning away the branches of questions that seem unimportant or repetitive. Technically, of course, such pruning makes the tree non-MECE, but that's okay. Remember, the whole purpose of tools is to get a job done, effectively and efficiently, so your goal is a tree that's *practically* MECE, not just *theoretically* MECE. A carefully pruned tree still forces you to apply rigorous logic to spot all the important possibilities, but it also "cuts to the chase."

Consider the following tree, adapted from our work with the fashion magazine whose story we told you earlier:

There's more than one way to cover a fashion trend.

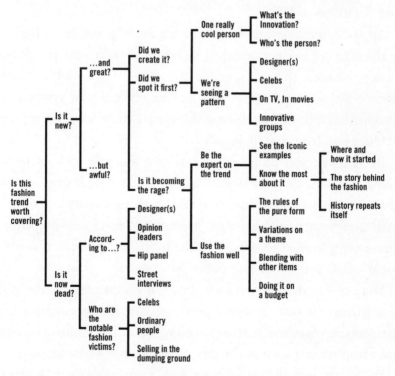

Figure 4.8: Logic Tree—Story Angles For A Fashion Trend

This tree provides the magazine with a useful "playbook" of the important story angles available to it in covering a fashion trend. But technically, it's not MECE. For example, its first two branches mention the birth and death of a fashion trend, but it omits any discussion of a fashion that's in the middle of its life cycle, or any discussion of perennial favorites, or those aspects of fashion that are permanent fixtures on the scene.

Is that okay? *Absolutely.* Because the magazine's previous experience showed that these stories were less interesting to its readers, it appropriately omitted them from the final version of the tree that was actually used to provide guidance to its staffers.

You should do the same. There's no reason to obfuscate the more helpful questions in your tree by burying them in a forest of theoretically existent but practically unhelpful branches, just to meet the technical definition of MECE.

Apply rigorous logic to spot all the important possibilities, but don't be afraid to cut to the chase. Just be careful—make sure you develop a more complete tree, then prune away the unimportant questions, versus simply "whipping off" a tree that reflects your conventional thinking but fails to stretch your thinking. (We're advocating practical efficiency, but not sloppiness!)

By the way, you probably noticed that this tree appears to stop asking questions about halfway through its branches. Is that okay too? *Absolutely.* A "question" doesn't always have to end with a question mark. You're not a contestant on *Jeopardy*—so don't feel compelled to phrase every avenue of inquiry in the form of a question if doing so would simply make your tree clumsier.

You can design logic trees for almost any ideation task. We've designed them for new products, processes, service improvements, investments, competitive strategies, you name it. Trees should be a core tool whenever you want to search systematically for new ideas.

We're often asked, "How far out should you take a tree? How many layers should a perfect tree contain?" After all, you could keep breaking each subbranch into more and more subquestions, driving yourself crazy in the process. Or you could stop very quickly and be left with a question that's so patently obvious you wonder why you needed a tree to discover it. (Yes, we've actually seen trees where the most specific question was "How do we increase profits?")

As always, there is no magic answer—it's a judgment call. But fortunately, the criteria for making your judgment are straightforward (and similar to the criteria for a good question that we described in Chapter 2). The end branches on your tree should provide very specific guidance to your thinking, while still allowing for some reasonable variety of good answers—in other words, if there are only one or two good answers to a question at the far end of your tree, you've gone too far. In our experience, the sweet spot tends to occur in the third to fifth layers of the tree, and tends to occur when the tree has between twenty-five and fifty branches in total.

To illustrate, look at the dilemma faced by those TV shows that dote on Hollywood actors and actresses. It's a crowded market—there's *Entertainment Tonight*, *Access Hollywood*, *TMZ on TV*, *Extra*, and *The Insider*, to name just a few. There's even a full-time cable network, E! Entertainment Television, devoted to the subject. And that doesn't even count the part-time celebrity followers like the network morning shows or CNN. Or the hundreds of Internet sites devoted to the same subject.

In short, there's more airtime to fill across all of these shows than there are discrete celebrity events to fill it. That means each show needs to find a different and unique aspect of each event to report on.

So how many "real stories" or "stories behind the story" can be derived from a single celebrity news event? Here's a tree that shows major story angles those TV shows could use to make hay out of any celebrity news event that might occur—from Lindsay having yet another car accident, to Jennifer finally reconciling with Brad, to Meryl winning her third Academy Award:

"You've heard the story...now hear the *real* story!"

Figure 4.9: Logic Tree—Story Angles For A Celebrity Event

As the examples in this chapter illustrate, logic trees can be helpful in an amazingly broad cross section of situations. We literally use them every day or two, whether identifying new lines of business for an Internet entrepreneur, developing new products for a medium-size retail bank, or identifying ways to cut overhead expenses at a multibillion-dollar restaurant chain.

So get out there and try them. After a short time, you'll find they simply become second nature—and they'll help you identify more questions and ideas than you could ever have imagined using only your intuition.

5

The Right (and Wrong) Uses of Analysis in Ideation

In our view, one of the least productive debates about how best to develop new ideas is the false dichotomy that's often drawn between "being creative" and "being analytical." Academics, professional facilitators, and career counselors alike have fueled the idea that, because some mental functions take place in the right hemisphere of the brain and others take place in the left, people cannot be both creative and analytical at the same time.

In our view, creativity and analysis are intertwined. We don't subscribe to the idea that you have to choose between a "right-brain perspective" and a "left-brain perspective." In our experience, the best approach—the Brainsteering approach—is to continually jump back and forth between them, using both the creative "right-brain perspective" *and* the analytical "left-brain perspective." Sometimes your ideation process will originate from a purely creative insight or query, sometimes from an analytical finding. No matter where it starts, you'll maximize your odds of success if you constantly go back and forth between the two perspectives. For example, you might select a Right Question, hit on an idea, assess it from an analytical perspective in the most rudimentary way for just a few seconds, refine it, test it again in more depth, and so on, improving your idea each step of the way.

In reality, most truly creative ideas require the inventor to move back and forth between the two perspectives. Would Michael Dell's idea to bypass retailers have gotten very far if he hadn't been analytical enough to calculate that the substantial distribution cost savings would enable his smaller company to sell its computers at a huge discount versus those of its competitors? Would the three founders of Compaq have quit their day jobs at Texas Instruments if their analysis showed that a portable computer could not be made at an acceptable cost? You know the answer.

CREATORS OF NEW IDEAS IGNORE ANALYSIS AT THEIR PERIL

The time was 1984. Federal Express had already achieved spectacular business success by dramatically reducing the time necessary to move a package across the country from the previous norm of several days (via the U.S. Postal Service) to overnight (via FedEx).

Buoyed by its success, FedEx decided to reduce delivery time even further. It noticed that a portion of its volume consisted of small packets of printed material in which the important item being transported was the information or image on the page, not the paper document itself. At that time, the only facsimile machines (as they were called back then) were expensive, unreliable, and slow—each page had to be individually attached to a rotating drum, and each page took several minutes to transmit.

So FedEx initiated a service called ZapMail, which guaranteed delivery among major cities within a then astoundingly short time of just two hours. The customer would drop off his material at a FedEx site, from which the company would send an electronic facsimile of the material to another FedEx site located near the intended recipient. A FedEx courier would then package the newly printed material in a special envelope and hand-carry it to its final destination.

The service was both capital intensive and labor intensive. FedEx needed physical offices near both the senders and recipients of documents. It needed staff members waiting on one end to accept a submission and transmit it, and on the other end to receive and deliver it.

We don't know how much analysis FedEx devoted to designing the in-house systems required to create ZapMail, but it's entirely obvious that the company failed to devote enough analysis to fully understand the technology trends regarding facsimile equipment. The entire, expensive ZapMail system—the offices, the staffing, the nice sheets of paper, the impressive ZapMail packages, the billing system—was designed around the premise that facsimile machines would remain too expensive for individual businesses and consumers to purchase for their own use. But within just a few months of ZapMail's debut, that assumption proved spectacularly wrong. The prices of fax machines (as they soon came to be called) fell dramatically, even as their reliability and ease of use rose equally dramatically. Every business with any significant need for instant transmittal of data or images could buy a fax machine for itself—and very soon consumers could, too.

The bottom line? FedEx lost over $200 million in operating Zap-Mail and another $320 million in the shutdown process (and in 1986, $520 million was a still lot of money).[1]

FedEx should have seen it coming. Given how quickly cheaper fax machines arrived on the market after ZapMail began operations, it's clear that the very technology that destroyed ZapMail was already far along in its development process at the time of ZapMail's launch. It's equally clear that FedEx must have been in contact with fax machine manufacturers—after all, it had to purchase similar machines for its own FedEx locations. The company simply failed to conduct an easy but crucial analysis.

ANALYSIS IS *ALWAYS* NECESSARY

We can hear some of you now: "Okay, I get the need for analysis in starting a big business. But I don't need it in my situation—my work is purely creative." But alas, you're wrong. The requirement to move back and forth between creativity and analysis doesn't apply only to ideas in the field of business. It applies to ideas in all kinds of fields—even those that are typically stereotyped as being purely "right brained," such as the arts. For example, would you like to write scripts for television? If so, get ready to conduct a lot of analysis.

First, of course, you need a great idea for your TV show—but not the kind you might think. It's not a plot idea, because any one plot will be exhausted in a single episode, and the networks will purchase your show only if it can be built into a series. So the premise and the characters must form the center of your idea. But wait: the premise and the characters must operate within some very stringent constraints. The premise must be targeted at an attractive audience that's not already overserved (analysis), and the range of characters must appeal to various subsegments of that target audience (analysis). The premise, the characters, and the settings those characters are placed in must be ones that your show's production budget can afford within the confines of the price that the networks are willing to pay for it (*lots* of analysis).

Still interested in chasing that Emmy Award? You're just getting started. What's the format and genre of your show? Each format and genre—say, a half-hour sitcom, or a one-hour drama—has additional analytical rules within which your "pure creativity" must function. For example, any episode of a one-hour drama on network TV must last *exactly* forty-four minutes, and since the other sixteen minutes are for commercials, it is not okay to have an episode last forty-four minutes and fifteen seconds. It takes analysis to make each episode fit precisely.

Actually, come to think of it, forty-four minutes isn't really the critical restriction. The critical restriction is that each episode must have six segments, each of which is between six and seven minutes long, that collectively add up to exactly forty-four minutes (analysis). Oh—and each of the first five segments must end with a dramatic cliff-hanger to make sure the audience will return to their seats before the show returns from commercial (more analysis).

Now comes the requirement to have both an "A story" and a "B story"—two different but intertwined plot lines that can be used to appeal to different segments of the audience—in each episode, and there are rules about how much time should be devoted to each story (more analysis). Then there are plot arcs, character arcs, and even intrascene arcs to worry about (each of which involves analysis).

And as soon as your series enters its second episode, you have to worry about cross-episode and cross-season continuity (lots of analysis). After all, your audience will revolt if, in episode thirty-four, your hero fondly remembers snowball fights in college, when way back in episode six, he mentioned that his alma mater was the University of Florida. Or if he mentions that his saintly mother was an only child—but we met his maternal cousins for two minutes in one forgettable episode three seasons ago.

Think the TV example is unique? Not at all; the same issues are true in all forms of applied art. You'd face variations of these same constraints—and therefore have to do similar levels of analysis—if you were trying to write a Grammy-winning song or a *New York Times* best seller. Want to be a joke writer? You'd be amazed at the amount of structure (read: analysis) that actually goes into fashioning a single monologue for a late-night talk show host.

In fact, analysis lies beneath "pure art" as well. Consider the work of an iconic artist whose creations are often held up as examples of purely creative work: Jackson Pollock. Mr. Pollock was an American painter of the mid-twentieth century who was considered a major figure in the abstract expressionist movement. Abstract expressionist paintings try not to portray anything in particular—they are paintings not of a landscape, or of a young woman, or *of* anything else. They're the ones that often elicit the supposition, "My five-year-old could have painted that." Mr. Pollock's works in particular draw that snarky comment, because his best-known paintings consist solely of what seem to be random drippings of various colors onto the canvas. And it doesn't take much analysis to sling paint at a canvas.

Or does it? It turns out that Jackson Pollock's paintings are not random at all. In a study published in *Physics World* in June 1999, several authors found that many of Mr. Pollock's paintings clearly displayed the distinctly nonrandom properties of mathematical fractals, and that his works became more and more accurately fractal over time.[2]

In layperson's terms, Mr. Pollock didn't randomly sling paint at the canvas. If he had, some areas of his paintings would contain mostly red paint, others mostly blue, and so on. There would be big blotches and small. Instead, everything is surprisingly even—the drippings are of the same intensity everywhere, and each color appears evenly across the canvas. And in fulfillment of the mathematical fractal criterion, if you examine any subsection of the painting, you see that the pattern of the subsection matches the pattern of the entire painting.

So while the form of his analysis might have been less conventional than that used to structure a TV series, Mr. Pollock certainly blended in a healthy dose of analysis with his creativity.

Clearly, then, the issue is not creativity versus analysis—both are necessary if you want to be successful creatively.

But how do you conduct analysis in truly helpful ways, as opposed to the traditionally idea-blocking ways employed by most people? In our experience, analysis can be used in two highly productive ways: to originate new ideas and to evaluate new ideas. But these two uses are not the same, and therefore the "right analysis" means something different in each case.

USING ANALYSIS TO ORIGINATE NEW IDEAS

Opportunities and ideas can often be found through analysis—but not the kind of analysis they usually teach in business school.

In business school, you're taught a standard set of analyses that you perform on off-the-shelf databases—collections of facts and figures created by those who came before you—to understand what's going on in your particular industry, company, or field of endeavor. Things like industry analyses compiled by Wall Street investment firms, market research reports on consumer laundry habits compiled by Procter & Gamble, or daily sales reports showing how much merchandise moved off the shelves yesterday at each of the 1,043 Victoria's Secret stores around the nation.[3]

Once they graduate, MBAs typically continue to look for such existing databases. But think about this approach for a second: if an idea can be found by applying conventional analytical techniques to existing databases, why haven't any of the thousands of searchers that preceded you already found the idea? And think about the limitations of analyzing existing databases. For a database to be useful, its developer must array the data in whatever form will be most useful to existing users—and that means, by definition, the data will always be arranged to facilitate insights about whatever is the existing way of thinking, not a new way.

The net result of all this leads to the Coyne Brothers' Principle of Preexisting Databases: "The more innovative an idea is, the less likely it is to have been derived from conventional analysis of historical data and events." (Feel free to quote it by name. If it gets popular enough, we'll print it on coffee mugs.)

So what can you do different from everyone else to find the insights they've missed? In a phrase: *use analysis to look for anomalies.* That means ferreting out those numbers, ratios, and calculations that others haven't thought of, in order to discover where things are *not* average. Where conditions have changed since the status quo was established. Where some efforts pay off highly, while other seemingly similar efforts fail to produce a return at all. And, perhaps most important, where "good" hides the potential for "great."

The Brainsteering approach to analysis exploits two tendencies that cause most people to miss certain kinds of insights. The first tendency is to be biased toward believing that any well-functioning process doesn't bear questioning. For most people, the world functions reasonably smoothly most of the time, because most things fit into patterns and those patterns make sense to them. These people "learned" at a young age that most attempts to try something different weren't worth the investment of effort, or the risk. They "learned" that the best way to do things today is probably about the same as it was yesterday. They "learned" that if a system is functioning well, there's probably little scope for significant improvement. Only those things that are obviously broken—whether they be ideas, products, or processes—deserve much effort to fix them.

The second tendency is to simplify a complex world through norms and averages. People's lives are complicated. In fact, every element of their lives seems complicated. (Have you ever tried to learn all the different things your cell phone can do? Wow, it's complicated—and it's just your cell phone!) So people usually make a simplifying assumption: that everything in a particular field behaves about like the average. If there are many customers, their behavior can probably be understood by looking at the average customer. If there are many tasks to be performed, and the collective value of all the tasks exceeds their collective cost by 20 percent, then the value of each task probably exceeds its cost by about 20 percent. If customers in aggregate are willing to pay a 10 percent premium for our product, then all customers individually are probably willing to pay a 10 percent premium.

As you can already tell, both these tendencies are unproductive, and if you can avoid them, you'll have given yourself a big head start in the race to identify breakthrough ideas. Let's look at some examples of how using analysis to look for anomalies has helped people find breakthrough ideas in situations where you might reasonably have expected that all the best opportunities had already been discovered.

Major League Baseball is probably the last place you might expect that there would be untapped potential for analysis. After all, the game has been played professionally since 1869, and thousands of amateur and professional statisticians have tracked the game in excruciating detail for over a century.

According to the book *Moneyball: The Art of Winning an Unfair Game*, Billy Beane, the general manager of the American League's Oakland A's since 1997, faced a difficult problem early in his tenure, one shared by many teams in smaller markets: he just couldn't afford to pay as much as other clubs to get the "best" players.[4]

However, it turns out that the traditional statistics used to track players' performance (and thereby determine which players were the "best")—statistics such as batting averages, fielding errors, and earned run averages—were flawed indicators of actual (past) performance. Take just one of those statistics: batting average. A player's batting average treats a walk as if it didn't exist—but in fact, in most cases a walk is as good as a single, so shouldn't it count for something? Further, batting average gives no more credit to a home run than to a single—but surely a home run is more valuable and represents a far better performance by the batter.

So a little-known—but better—set of statistics emerged. Pioneered by a baseball historian and statistician named Bill James, these new statistics were collectively referred to as "sabermetrics."

Billy Beane and his organization developed an interesting analysis. They asked, "Are there players whose performance scores well when judged by sabermetrics (and who, therefore, are truly high performers), but scores poorly when judged by traditional statistics (and who, therefore, are believed by more conventional teams to be only mediocre performers)?" If so, these players would be highly effective but would not be highly sought after by the majority of other clubs—and would therefore represent an unusual bargain.

As it turned out, there were many such players, which enabled Mr. Beane and his Oakland colleagues to create a team that performed as well as the top-paid teams in all of the major leagues—at less than half the cost of the most expensive teams.

Oakland's so-called Moneyball philosophy was eventually adopted by several forward-thinking teams in both the American and National Leagues. Today, the Arizona Diamondbacks, Boston Red Sox,

Cleveland Indians, New York Mets, New York Yankees, San Diego Padres, St. Louis Cardinals, Toronto Blue Jays, and Washington Nationals all have full-time sabermetrics analysts on staff.

A second classic example of using analysis to successfully generate new ideas occurred in the multibillion-dollar credit card industry, where one executive and his team found an obvious hole that all its competitors had overlooked.

Banks are generally happy if they make 1 percent net profit between their own cost of borrowing money and the net interest they earn from turning around and lending that same money to borrowers (after subtracting their costs of running the business and any loan losses, of course). So, for example, in 1975 the simplified profit equation for a typical credit card bank might have looked like this: (1) borrow funds at a 9 percent interest rate but charge 13 percent on the loans, creating a 4 percent spread; (2) budget for 1 percent costs to acquire new customers and another 1 percent to run the operations (such as processing transactions and sending statements); (3) make sure loan losses remain below 1 percent; and (4) voilà! a net profit of 1 percent.

However, credit card banks had to be careful. If loan losses crept up even slightly from 1 percent to 2 percent, the bank would no longer make money. So every bank had a chief credit officer whose job was to minimize write-offs. And how do you minimize write-offs? You grant credit only to those people whom you believe are *really* likely—as in, 99 percent likely—to pay it back. That's exactly what banks did—and the system worked well.

Beginning in the late 1970s, interest rates spiked to around 18 percent. The banks had to pay more interest on the money they borrowed, so they raised the rates on the money they lent to credit card users to about 22 percent—and the spread remained at its historical 4 percent level while the net profit remained at its historical 1 percent level.

Here's where it gets interesting. Beginning in 1981, interest rates started coming down, falling to about 12 percent within a year. But instead of lowering the rates they charged credit card customers, the banks kept those rates high—so now, instead of earning only the traditional 1 percent that would have kept them happy, credit card loans began earning five or six times that amount! And because customers were paying the same interest rates they'd gotten used to, they kept using those cards.

About that time, Citibank decided for obvious reasons that it wanted to grow the credit card business, and grow it quickly. A bright executive named John Reed and his team conducted a simple analysis. They looked back at that profit equation we described above. The cost of borrowing had fallen to 12 percent, while the rates the banks charged customers had stayed at 22 percent. That gave them a 10 percent spread to run the operation. Operating costs had stayed about 1 percent, leaving 9 percent to cover customer acquisition expenses and loan losses.

Citibank could afford to raise its spending on acquiring more customers who were at least 99 percent likely to repay their loans—but that's what every other bank was doing. Instead, Reed's team decided to focus on a new group of customers: those who just barely failed the "99 percent test." That is, instead of being one of many banks offering a credit card to households with a 1 percent or less chance of defaulting, Citibank could be the *only* bank offering cards to those households who had somewhere between a 1 percent and 2 percent chance of defaulting. The equation would still work fine—after all, 10 percent spread minus 1 percent operating costs, minus another 1 to 2 percent acquisition costs and 2 percent loan losses, still yields an enviable 5 percent net profit—and Citibank would be earning that 5 percent on a much larger base of business.

That's just what Citibank did. It took a lot of analysis—and courage, particularly when the first attempt to loosen credit standards went poorly and the bank lost hundreds of millions of dollars one year—but that strategy drove a massive, and massively profitable, expansion of Citibank's credit card business for the rest of the decade.

In both the Moneyball and Citibank cases, the vast majority of players in a huge industry missed major opportunities because they failed to look for the anomaly—the quirky difference, the reason why good might be different from great, the place where the averages masked the unique.

(Note, however, that Citibank's core idea worked well when only one institution pursued it after careful consideration, but terribly when too many institutions later pursued an analogous idea without careful consideration. In the mortgage market of the early and mid-2000s, more and more banks piled into subprime lending, credit standards became progressively looser and looser, eventually causing the world-wide financial crisis of 2008 and the "Great Recession" that followed. When your analysis and your insight are original and thoroughly considered, good things usually follow; but even a great idea, when chased by many others without thoughtful examination, can lead to disaster.)

We're not exaggerating when we say that we have *never* had an assignment where anomalies didn't exist. But to find them, your analysis must be the right kind. Listen for the unusual, the unexplained, the unexplored. Be on guard whenever anyone utters phrases like "everyone knows," or "we've always looked at it that way," or "that's just how it's done around here." Then ask yourself where things might not be so average, where conditions might have changed, where other people just assume that the current system is good enough. That's where, and how, you'll be able to target your analysis to find possibilities. And when your left brain finds the right anomaly, your right brain will find a great idea.

USING ANALYSIS TO EVALUATE NEW IDEAS

Everyone has a pet peeve. Some people have treasure troves of them. In our careers as consultants, one of our pet peeves is when a client asks us to "develop a new, innovative, completely unique strategy—a real breakthrough!" and then, when we've come up with one, tells us they won't act on the new strategy unless we can point to three or four companies that have already succeeded with that very strategy.

There's an obvious but overlooked trade-off between the original-ity of an idea and the level of historical precedent that one can find for it. You'll never implement a truly new idea if you demand absolute proof of its success before you start.

Does that mean you should take the opposite approach: evaluating new ideas in a data-free environment, just guessing what might work? Of course not. There's a long history of spectacular business failures that could easily have been avoided by paying just a little bit of atten-tion to some very basic facts.

This section focuses on finding the right balance between asking new questions, asking old questions, and failing to ask some obvious questions altogether. Since that last possibility can be particularly wasteful, let's start there. At the beginning of this chapter, we de-scribed the problems of ZapMail's analysis (or lack thereof). But Zap-Mail is hardly alone in this regard.

Take the case of Webvan, a much-hyped idea during the dot-com era of the late 1990s. The idea was simple: a customer would order groceries over the Internet, and those groceries would be delivered to her home. Moreover, the concept had already been proved to work in at least one instance: a small company named Peapod had implemented a similar idea very successfully in a small section of the San Francisco area. Slam dunk, right?

Webvan raised over $1 billion from leading venture capitalists, and even hired away the CEO of Andersen Consulting (an enormous and prestigious consulting firm, now known as Accenture) to be its CEO. Webvan's strategy was to build a gigantic warehouse in each city it served, receive all orders centrally, and dispatch all the delivery trucks from that one location. Further, Webvan decided to use a citywide marketing strategy, meaning that it would deliver groceries anywhere in a metropolitan area. Webvan began building out infrastructure in ten cities simultaneously, spending vast amounts each month.[5]

And yet Webvan's strategy contained three obvious and fatal flaws, ones that we and others spotted before their operations even began.

Flaw #1

Let's do a little arithmetic. Take Atlanta, one of Webvan's initial roll-out cities, as an example. The diameter of the greater Atlanta metropolitan area is over seventy miles. Webvan would need a fleet of trucks, half of which would have to drive to the far side of Atlanta to begin their delivery routes , then all the way back to Webvan's one warehouse at the end of each shift. Averaging together the nearby delivery routes and the faraway delivery routes, Webvan would lose over an hour per day per truck, and put seventy miles on each truck, just getting each truck to and from the starting point of its delivery route. If we assume that their average truck costs $1.25 per mile to operate, and that its driver costs $15 an hour (including benefits), that's $102 of overhead per truck per day—*before the truck makes its first delivery.*

Is that a lot? Let's think about how many deliveries a truck can make in a day. When the truck is "on station" and operating at full utilization, it can make perhaps five deliveries per hour—that is, assuming it takes twelve minutes to leave one house and drive to the next one, pull into the next house's driveway, ring the bell, wait for an answer, find the particular box containing that house's delivery, carry it in, return to the truck, look up the next delivery, and—in those days—find the next house on a map and plan the route.

Based on five deliveries per hour, a truck could make forty deliveries a day if it were on station eight hours a day and operating at full utilization. But wait: the driver needs bathroom breaks and time for lunch, so an eight-hour shift actually provides just six and a half hours of possible on-station time. In addition, Webvan's single-warehouse strategy takes away one of those hours (or 15 percent of its remaining capacity) as the truck gets to the starting point of its delivery route and returns home at the end of it, so there are only five and a half hours remaining. That means a truck can really make only twenty-seven deliveries per day.

And by the way, can the trucks actually operate at full utilization? Maybe, except that Webvan guaranteed a thirty-minute window for deliveries. So Webvan could not optimize its truck routes; it had to design routes that allowed trucks to be at specified places at specified times of the day. To see how this would destroy productivity, imagine that half of all customers specified a noon delivery window and half specified a 2:00 p.m. delivery window. A truck could handle perhaps three customers in the noon window—and then it would have to wait around to handle three more around 2:00 p.m. In such a case, Webvan would need one truck for every six customers, and the truck would have nothing to do the rest of the day. Now, the real situation wouldn't be as extreme as our example, once Webvan had enough customers— but it was bad enough to cut productivity in half in the company's early days. And that means only 13.5 deliveries per day per truck.

Dividing the $102 overhead cost identified above by 13.5 deliveries per day means that Webvan's single-warehouse strategy would add $7.55 to the cost of every delivery. How much is $7.55? If a typical single order of groceries was worth, say, $60, and Webvan operated at typical grocery industry gross margins of 25 percent, that would generate $15 of gross margin to pay all of the company's operating expenses—the trucks, the warehouse, the ordering system, etc., etc.

So Webvan's plan used up over half of its entire gross margin *just getting trucks to and from their delivery areas* in the early days of its operation.

Flaw #2

Webvan's problems went even deeper, because the overall design of their business strategy meant that Webvan would incur almost its full set of operating costs from day one. It needed the full warehouse, and it needed to advertise across the entire city. Because it delivered everywhere, it needed the full fleet of trucks from day one—including sending a truck to the far side of Atlanta even if only a single customer asked for delivery that day. Meanwhile, however, Webvan's revenue stream would build up only slowly as customers gradually came to understand and accept Webvan's new approach to grocery-buying and change their purchase behavior accordingly (which any consumer marketer will tell you is never an easy thing for a company to accomplish in a short time). Therefore, Webvan would bleed cash for a substantial time in every city in which it launched.

Webvan should have seen these problems in advance. Every company that operates a delivery business knows that two of the largest profitability drivers (no pun intended this time) are (1) cost and time to get on station, and (2) route density.

Flaw #3

Finally, Webvan compounded its problems tenfold via one more strategic error. It could have chosen to "go live" in one city to learn firsthand whether a single-warehouse strategy was more efficient than having several smaller warehouses in a metropolitan area, each located closer to the actual delivery zone, and/or to learn whether its business model could develop enough customers quickly enough to solve the density problem. Instead, Webvan decided to launch in ten cities simultaneously—and pay the exorbitant cost of learning the same lessons ten times.

When the dust settled in 2001, Webvan was gone—and its investors lost almost every penny of their billion-dollar investment.

THE RIGHT ANALYSIS AT THE RIGHT TIME

In both the ZapMail and Webvan cases, we have to believe that many smart people spent many weeks on analysis—but blew it anyway. These people would probably defend themselves by saying, "You can't analyze everything. Wouldn't you drown in analysis, and never take any action, if you analyzed every idea to its fullest before proceeding?" Of course—but somehow, in each case, they failed to conduct even a relatively simple analysis of the *right* factors: the trajectory of the technology in ZapMail's case, and the basic operating economics in Webvan's case. Somehow they got lost in the weeds.

How do you avoid their fate? By matching the stage of your

analysis—including both the subjects you examine and the depth in which you examine them—to the development stage of your idea. There is a right set of analysis for each stage, one that makes it far less likely that you'll overlook something crucial while also preventing you from drowning in minutiae.

Depending on the development stage of your idea—whether it be for a new business or product, an improved work process, or a potential source of cost reduction—the Brainsteering approach to analysis requires you to examine your idea at one of four increasingly sophisticated stages: first blush, quick discovery, design on paper, and full-blown planning.

The four stages of analysis are designed to follow the principle of "causing the cheapest destruction first." That is, you should sequence your analysis in such a way that, if your idea is destined to fail at any point, it fails after you have spent the least possible time and effort, not the most. How do you accomplish this? At each stage of your idea's development, limit your analysis to a few core subjects that are critical to that stage, and don't waste your time making detailed prognostications about aspects of the idea—such as premature volume or revenue estimates—that you can't yet make with any reasonable degree of accuracy.

To illustrate the first three analytical stages (plenty of good books already exist on how to conduct full-blown planning efforts at the fourth stage), let's return to that idea we introduced back in Chapter 1 about delivering gasoline to people's cars. Let's call it "Gas-To-You."

When we left off, we had just asked: "Where and when are there consistently going to be many cars parked right next to each other for long periods of time? So many cars that, even if only one in ten or one in twenty cars needs gas that day, the next customer's car is easy for my truck driver to find and only a very short distance from the car he just filled?"

The obvious answer: large parking lots. And not just any large parking lots. Ideally, large parking lots to which the same cars return consistently (so that we can sign up a customer once and fill his car every time he needs it), and where the cars sit for a predictable, extended period (so that we have a wide window of time in which to catch and fill up the customer's car). That means office building and factory parking lots during the day, and apartment or condominium parking lots at night.

Quickly, the outline of the business begins to emerge. We reach exclusive deals with owners of the above parking lots. We sign up individual customers through one-time on-site campaigns, subsequent mailings, and a Web site. Formally signing up customers allows us to collect their credit card information and secure official permission to fill their cars. Each customer is given a large orange triangle to hang from his rearview mirror (or any of several equivalent indicators we could invent) on those days when he wants a fill-up. Our minitanker makes the rounds during the promised hours (such as "any time between 9:00 a.m. and noon for this particular office building"), filling up those cars that need it, and charging the appropriate credit card. (There are many other helpful details that aren't necessary to repeat here—like how to handle cars for which access to the gas tank requires flipping a lever inside the car—but you get the picture.)

So now let's do some analysis.

FIRST BLUSH ANALYSIS

What analysis should you do immediately? The kind that you can do in your head, on an intuitive basis, within just a minute or two (or, if you feel compelled to gather a few relevant facts first, within no more than two hours).

While you could go crazy analyzing everything, it would be a mistake at this stage to do so. There are just too many unknowns at this point to make any reasonable projections of market size, competition, costs, margins, and so on.

The good news is that you don't need to. At the first blush stage, you need only investigate five issues that, together, will effectively and efficiently give you a highly reliable initial indication as to whether or not the idea will be valuable. Those five issues are: fundamental plausibility, genuine value, size of affected target, obvious showstoppers, and explanation for the anomaly. Let's look at each in more detail.

Is the idea fundamentally plausible? Here, you visualize the idea in your head as if it were fully up and running. Don't even worry at this point about temporary start-up issues; that will come later, and only if your idea passes several other tests first—that's what we mean by "cheapest destruction first."

Does what you see make sense, or does it require too many changes in existing customer behavior? Or too specialized a set of circumstances to succeed? Or some technological breakthrough that doesn't yet exist and that you have no reasonable way of securing?

Gas-To-You seems fundamentally plausible. It's easy to imagine pickup-truck-size minitankers servicing cars in large parking lots. It's reasonable to believe that customers would pay at least as much for delivered gasoline as for similar-quality gasoline purchased at a traditional gas station. So the key question becomes whether the service would be too costly to provide.

A competitive cost structure seems fundamentally plausible. There is no new technology to invent. A quick visit to the Internet would suggest our minitankers could be built for about $80,000 each—a lot less than the multimillion-dollar cost of building a traditional gas station. The labor content would be about the same as having one full-time person sitting behind the counter at a self-service gas station, taking payments. If cars typically drive 15,000 miles a year and get 20 miles to the gallon, each car needs to be filled about once a week. If we sign up 20 percent of the cars in a given office building's parking lot and visit the lot five times a week, every twenty-fifth car will need filling each day. With cars parked on both sides of an aisle, the next fill-up is only twelve or thirteen cars away from the last one. At four minutes per car (including moving our minitanker the twelve or thirteen spaces) and fourteen gallons per fill, the little tanker can pump 210 gallons per hour—which a quick Google search indicates is more than the average gas station pumps in the same time period (because most of their pumps are not in use most of the time). So if we can find the right parking lots and sign up sufficient customers, the idea seems very plausible.

Does the idea add genuine value? To be truly successful, any idea must add genuine value. Not trivial value or fad value—such ideas, even successful ones like Chia Pets or the Snuggie, tend to succeed based more on luck than anything else (for example, as the result of a quirky sales pitch that happens to amuse people). If you're looking to get rich based on a fad, you might as well go out and buy a Powerball ticket.

No, to be truly successful over a sustained period of time, an idea must fill a strong customer need that is unfilled now, or else it must reduce costs significantly. If an idea adds genuine value, you'll most likely be able to find a way to make it pay off; if not, there probably won't be a way to make money with it, at least not for more than a short time (Inside-the-Shell Electric Egg Scrambler, anyone?).

Again, don't worry at this point about building complex Excel spreadsheets to predict your return on investment, or even trying to make detailed sales projections—that will come later, and only if your idea passes several other tests first. At this point, just ask yourself whether the idea would add genuine value by making a real difference for its users— and the more difference it would make to each user, the better.

As for Gas-To-You, remember from Chapter 1 that taking time to go to the gas station was the biggest hassle customers currently face. And how much more hassle is it to fill a car when it's freezing cold or raining outside? We just eliminated that hassle. At the first blush level, that seems compelling enough to get customers' attention.

What's the size of the affected target? Every new idea affects a "pool of economic activity," such as customer purchases of an existing product that your new invention will replace, or a set of routines that will enable workers to complete your new process in half the time at half the cost.

So ask yourself: "Does this idea affect a significant pool of economic activity—a large number of buyers, an existing product or service that's high volume or high value, certain activities that consume significant amounts of time or cost—or only a small pool?"

By combining this criterion with the previous one, we see that an idea that adds genuine value against a large affected target is an idea with high potential. (What an important point—we can see more coffee mugs being printed up any day now.)

Importantly, notice that we still recommend against trying to make any detailed estimate of market size at this stage; there simply isn't enough information available yet to make a useful estimate. After all, you don't want to be the next person to join the long line of people and organizations who infamously conducted studies that made premature (and ultimately ridiculous) assessments of market demand—such as the early study that showed the entire worldwide demand for computers would only ever be five units. Or the one that said that copy machines wouldn't succeed because no one would ever need more than three copies of any document (and therefore carbon paper would suffice). Or the one that said cell phones would flop. No, don't try to make up "reasonable" numbers at this stage. Just be satisfied using the simple standard, "adds genuine value against a large affected target."

In the case of Gas-To-You, we need to ask whether there are enough large parking lots, filled with cars on a regular basis, to create a large business, or whether the idea would make sense only under certain highly unusual circumstances. It's not hard to tell that this idea should have a lot of potential in every big city, but less potential in small towns. Fortunately, there are enough big cities in the United States to constitute a very large affected target—and therefore a highly attractive potential market.

Are there any screamingly obvious showstoppers that would instantly kill this idea? You'll need to think broadly—but not very deeply—at this stage. For example, if you're hoping to enter any kind of technology business, you should ask the obvious question: is there a technology already in the marketplace or under development that would render this idea obsolete? (By the way, we assume that you just flashed back to ZapMail's error.) Different kinds of businesses have different kinds of showstoppers.

Let's check back in on Gas-To-You: might gasoline-powered cars become obsolete? Don't worry, we've actually studied this question for a large oil company. Despite the hype, truly large-scale adoption of electric cars is still a long way off in the future due to all kinds of technological, infrastructure, and consumer behavior hurdles. Hydrogen-based cars? An absurdly long way off. Our idea is safe for at least a couple of decades. Is there something obviously illegal about the idea? Nope, nothing obvious.

What's the explanation for the anomaly? Even at this first blush stage of analysis, you should ask, "If this idea is so great, why hasn't someone else exploited it before? What puts me in a position to see something others haven't seen, or to be willing to act when others haven't been willing to act?"

Be careful: you have to walk a fine line here. On the one hand, you shouldn't blithely ignore historical precedents—Webvan was tragically arrogant in adopting a business model that flew in the face of every axiom observed by every delivery company on the planet.

On the other hand, though, you shouldn't simply assume that any new idea *must* be inherently flawed or else someone would already have done it. (In our experience, the worst offenders on this one are the "experts"; often, the more people know about how things are done today, the less open-minded they are about whether it can be done a better way.) There are real reasons why others might not see a great idea, or might choose not to pursue it. In fact, in the book *Innovation: The Attacker's Advantage* (that we first introduced to you back in Chapter 2), Richard Foster shows that the more successful a company has been with the current way of doing things, the less likely it will be to adopt the new way—even though odds are, it is actually the most likely company to have discovered the new way in the first place.

So just force yourself to answer the question, evenhandedly and explicitly, as in: "I believe that current player X has not pursued this idea because . . ." See if the explanation seems both plausible and convincing to you. That's enough for first blush.

Why haven't the major oil companies already pursued Gas-To-You? Because the major oil companies aren't interested in expanding their network of company-owned retail outlets. They consider retail outlets to be a money-losing business compared to their more profitable exploration and drilling activities. They prefer to sell their brand of gasoline through independent retailers—like we'd be. Meanwhile, the larger chains of retailers believe they still have plenty of room to build out more of their conventional stores—so they don't believe they need a new idea.

Okay, let's say your idea passes first blush. Now it merits just a few days to peel the onion by another layer or two—that is, to go through the stage of quick discovery.

QUICK DISCOVERY

In this stage, you'll again face the temptation to go crazy with analysis. Resist it. Instead, concentrate on four issues: performance requirements versus potential, critical assumptions, more showstoppers, and verifying the anomaly. Let's briefly consider each one.

Are the performance requirements that the idea *must* achieve to be successful compatible with reasonable expectations of what it *can* achieve? This question may sound both obvious and complicated, but it is neither. Start with the first part of the comparison, the performance requirements. As we mentioned above, an idea has to add genuine value in order to be adopted. This question asks you to estimate—just roughly—the degree of added value that will be necessary for you to succeed. If the idea is for a new product, how much better does the new product have to perform compared to existing ones in order to get customers to switch? If the idea is intended to reduce costs in order to be able to reduce prices, then how much of a reduction in price would be required to make customers switch? Would it be worth pursuing a cost reduction idea that saves $10,000, or only ones that save $100,000?

Be careful before declaring that your idea passes the performance requirements versus potential test. In a 2006 *Harvard Business Review* article entitled "Eager Sellers and Stony Buyers," Professor John Gourville wrote, "Consumers overvalue the existing benefits of an entrenched product by a factor of three, while developers overvalue the new benefits of their innovation by a factor of three. The result is a mismatch of nine to one, or 9×, between what innovators think consumers desire, and what consumers really want."[6] While Professor Gourville's arithmetic is overly simplistic (otherwise the average product would achieve only 11 percent of its predicted level sales—and we've been involved with enough product launches to know that's not quite true), his point is entirely legitimate. Most inventors of new ideas inherently believe their idea is more powerful than it actually is.

In the case of Gas-To-You, a quick set of focus groups confirm that a broad cross section of enthusiastic potential customers exists, at least enough to pass muster in the quick discovery phase. Further, they reveal that the complete set of performance specs includes a number of items that you might not think of right away. The service would clearly have to be safe, or the owners of the parking lots wouldn't grant us access. It would have to be reliable, or our customers would quickly abandon us. That means we must have enough minitankers to be able to visit every car in every lot as often as promised, even on days when we're very busy—and that we must make the rounds even on days when it doesn't seem to be worthwhile. So if everyone seems to want to fill up their cars on Mondays (after driving a lot over the weekend) or Fridays (in preparation for the next weekend), but no one wants to fill up on Tuesday (after all, they may have just filled up the day before), we have to find a way to deal with it. What's more, we have to keep the price of our gasoline close to what our customers would pay if they visited a traditional gas station. Otherwise, they'll use our service only as a backup, rather than using it for all their fill-ups, and our utilization ratios—and profitability—would be destroyed.

Next, independent of analyzing what's required, analyze what appears to be achievable. And not just under ideal conditions, but under real world conditions. How much worse is your average actual performance likely to be, considering that you'll have to operate even when volume is low, or when competition is tough, or when the weather is lousy. (Oops. We see Webvan again.) Time to build a few (simple!) spreadsheets.

For Gas-To-You, a small family of simple spreadsheets—modeling single parking lot economics, then single minitanker/single shift economics, then single refueling depot economics, and finally city level economics—shows the concept continues to work quite well so far.

What critical assumptions must prove to be accurate in order for the idea to succeed? Remember, you don't really know anything yet. Your initial analysis at this early stage is based on certain theoretical assumptions you've made and abstract data you've pulled from public and/or indirect sources, not on actual operating data. Therefore, you need to make a list of your assumptions in order to verify or refute them (which you'll invest time to do later, if the idea passes this stage of analysis).

The Gas-To-You concept works well—provided that the trucks are well utilized. Too much downtime, and the model falls apart. Too much time moving between cars, or driving back to the depot to refuel our minitankers, and the model falls apart. And so on. That finding helps us understand where to invest our efforts to verify or refute our critical assumptions—like utilization rates—in the next stage.

Are there any less obvious showstoppers that would kill the idea? In the first blush stage of analysis, it was sufficient to ask only about obvious showstoppers, ones that even a novice could spot. At this stage, you've learned more about your idea, and you may recognize new potential showstoppers—after all, you're not a novice anymore. But at this point, it's worth reaching out to others who have more knowledge than you do about the field in which you hope to apply your idea, to see if they see any showstoppers.

Obviously, you'll be careful not to divulge any secrets to someone who can steal them from you. But that's the easy part. The harder part is deciding when to listen to the experts' reactions and when to take them with a grain of salt or even ignore them completely. (Remember our earlier caution about experts and their frequent lack of open-mindedness?) You should expect the expert to tell you how bad your idea is and then to point out any number of showstoppers from his point of view. Your job will be to listen, think objectively and non-defensively, then decide whether you believe the showstoppers are real.

A couple of casual conversations with the owner of the local QuikTrip station, followed by a phone call to an old friend whose family owns about two dozen gas stations and buys its gasoline wholesale from one of the big oil companies, and still no showstoppers for Gas-To-You.

Does your explanation for the anomaly hold up under expert scrutiny? In the first blush stage of analysis, you relied purely on your own knowledge and logic to address the question of why your new idea doesn't already exist. Now is the time to invest the effort to find out those answers more definitively, by asking the experts. So as you listen to the experts' views on showstoppers above, also ask for any stories they might have about others who've tried the idea and what became of them.

Based on the knowledge of the experts consulted above, the primary reasons that Gas-To-You hasn't been tried before are precisely the ones identified earlier.

Idea still looking good? Then it's time to move to the next stage of analysis.

DESIGN ON PAPER

You may actually conduct this exercise several times, each time at an ever-increasing level of detail.

Here is where you invest the time and money to test the critical assumptions, in a particular order. Remember our principle: cheapest destruction first. Some assumptions are inexpensive to test, some very expensive. Some assumptions have more effect on the viability of your idea, some less. Some assumptions you're very confident about, others less so. Ideally, the assumption you'd test first would be the one that's least expensive, that also happens to have the deadliest consequences, and that you really have to admit you just pulled out of thin air. In real life, of course, Murphy's Law means you'll never be lucky enough to have one single assumption top the list on all three criteria, but you get the picture.

As you go through the process of testing your assumptions, you'll naturally begin to flesh out more and more details of your idea. You'll verify the marketplace's receptivity to your idea via (now very constructive) market research, build increasingly sophisticated financial and operating plans, conduct legal investigations, and so on. The details could fill a book, but you know how to take it from here.

Oh, by the way: Wondering what became of Gas-To-Go? You say you haven't noticed a fleet of cheerfully logo'd, friendly looking, pickup-truck-sized minitankers on the streets of your city?

Well, remember the concept of showstoppers? Early in the design on paper phase, we invested in some detailed legal and regulatory research. The basic concept of Gas-To-Go is indeed legal—but, as it turns out, fire code regulations in most states would prohibit the minitankers from entering enclosed parking decks, which dramatically lowers the economic attractiveness of the idea by putting many of the most productive parking lots off-limits to the service. While the minitankers themselves can, of course, be made quite safe, many fire commissioners worry that certain occupants of the office buildings—those taking a smoking break—might insist on coming over to our courteous, uniformed attendant to say hi. Lighted cigarettes and gasoline are a bad combination, of course—and although the commissioners agree that 99 percent of smokers would probably have the good sense to stay away, it takes only one idiot.

But we're still thinking about the idea. After all, we still like the idea of avoiding airport hassles with one of those private jets.

6

Optimizing Your Personal Ideation Performance

Sometimes you just get lucky. You're in the right place at the right time with the right question, and a great idea comes easily. In 1981 James Foster, an NFL executive, attended an indoor soccer game. He asked himself how football could be adapted to be played in an indoor arena—and the answer came to him then and there. While still at the game, he wrote his idea on a business envelope pulled from his briefcase, complete with rules, sketches of the field, and notes on game play. The eventual result was the Arena Football League, which has averaged attendance of 10,000 to 13,000 per game for over two decades, has been regularly broadcast on ESPN, and has spawned several video games.[1] (That said, the league has experienced rocky financials at different times over the years—pointing, once again, to the need for balancing creativity and analysis.)

More often than not, however, ideas don't "just hit you." You have to work to find them. The first part of this book taught you to ask Right Questions. This chapter builds on that foundation by helping you strengthen your ability to *answer* Right Questions. And as a bonus, we'll help you create a contingency approach for handling that sudden, unexpected moment when you, and you alone, have to come up with a great idea on the fly, at the wrong time and in the wrong place.

Applied sports psychology literature makes many references to players being "in the zone." The zone is a state in which an athlete performs to the best of his or her abilities—a sort of pinnacle of personal achievement. In the words of U.S. Olympic Team sports psychologist and researcher Shane Murphy, the zone is a "special place where performance is exceptional and consistent, automatic and flowing. An athlete is able to ignore all the pressures and let his or her body deliver the performance that has been learned so well. Competition is fun and exciting."[2]

In our experience, the same phenomenon holds in idea generation. The most creative people sometimes find themselves in a state of intense concentration, where great ideas seem to flow freely. They seem to live inside the task, visualizing a situation and the various innovations that could come out of it. In fact, their visualizations are sometimes so real that they can (and do) "automatically" see the many operational details involved, as if the innovation were already there in front of them, actually performing its function in real life. You've probably experienced this yourself, at least on occasion.

The big leap in your idea-generation skills—the one that would create a quantum leap in your ability to answer Right Questions— would be to get yourself into the zone *every time*. How do you dramatically improve your odds of doing so? Through four sets of actions:

Understanding the impact of emotions on creativity, and using this knowledge to your advantage

Neutralizing emotional overhead

Understanding your personal response to intrinsic and extrinsic motivations

Tailoring the idea-generation process to your personal style

UNDERSTANDING THE IMPACT OF EMOTIONS ON CREATIVITY

No one who's had to be consistently creative would be surprised to learn that your emotional state affects your ability to be creative.

However, the particular types of impact that your emotions can have are not necessarily the ones you'd expect. Further, there's actually been a bit of a reversal in the last few years in the prescriptions that science would offer you about how to use emotions to your advantage.

In 1999, one group of psychologists stated confidently, "It is now well recognized that positive affect leads to greater cognitive flexibility and facilitates creative problem solving across a wide range of circumstances."[3] Translated from academic-speak into plain English, they seemed to be saying, "If you want to be creative, be sure you're in a good mood." For many years, that message seemed to rule mainstream thinking, including being taught in business schools and spread by various gurus of creativity.

The problem was that before too long, contradictory evidence emerged. As one later scientific paper put it, "Indeed, whereas some studies suggest that positive mood states trigger more creativity than do negative mood states, other studies report similar levels of creativity, and still other studies report that negative moods promote creative performance more than do positive or neutral moods."[4]

Hmmm. So much for easy advice.

Fortunately, science has continued to make progress and academia now seems to be able to reconcile previous contradictions. Here's how the latest thinking goes: First, it's too simplistic to look at emotions as being only positive or negative. (By the way, if you'd like to impress your friends, positive and negative emotional states are referred to in the literature as "hedonic tones." Don't feel bad—we didn't know that either.) Second, you can't just look at your hedonic tone; you also need to look at the activation level of the emotion.

Basically, "activation" (and its synonym in the academic literature, "arousal") refers to your energy level. As one paper put it, "Low levels of arousal lead to inactivity and avoidance, neglect of information, and low cognitive . . . performance. . . . However, at moderate levels of arousal, individuals will be motivated to seek and integrate information and to consider multiple alternatives. . . . Activating mood states are thus more likely than deactivating mood states to increase attention to, and integration of, information."[5]

Given that explanation, you just know you want to be in an *activating mood state.*

But what about the ol' hedonic tone? (See how easily it just rolls off your tongue now?) Both positive and negative mood states work—but differently. Creativity can come from either exploring a broad cross section of possible solutions at a certain level of depth (referred to in the literature as "enhanced cognitive flexibility") or by really digging in and finding all the possibilities in a narrower subset of solutions (referred to as "enhanced persistence and perseverance"). In a nutshell, positive activating mood states help you do the former, whereas negative activating mood states help you do the latter.

So, if you want to think broadly, you should do so when you're happy, even elated (not calm and relaxed, as those are deactivating positive mood states). And if you want to really drill down on the nearby possibilities, a little anger or fear might help (although sadness or depression would not).

Just to prove we aren't making this stuff up, here's the specific quote from the paper:

[I]t follows that activating moods that are positive in tone increase creative fluency and originality primarily through enhanced cognitive flexibility, whereas activating moods that are negative in tone increase creative fluency and originality primarily through enhanced persistence and perseverance. Put differently, whereas we would not necessarily expect differences in creative fluency and originality between activating positive (such as happy, elated) moods and activating negative (such as angry, fearful) moods, we would expect activating positive moods to associate with broader and more inclusive cognitive categories, with greater diversity in the cognitive categories used to generate ideas, and with fast completion times in creative insight tasks. Vice versa, we would expect activating negative moods to associate with more ideas within specific cognitive categories and with relatively long completion times in creative insight tasks.[6]

See? Just like we said. Almost.

NEUTRALIZING EMOTIONAL OVERHEAD

There is one other key finding from the latest scientific research that reinforces an important phenomenon we had observed in our own work on creativity over the years: you cannot get into the zone, creatively speaking, if you're carrying too much "emotional overhead."

Most people can shut out distractions that remain mostly intellectual in nature, but fewer people can shut out distractions that, for them, have too large an emotional component. If something is strongly affecting your emotions—either positively or negatively—your production of neurochemicals (such as serotonin and dopamine) seems to compel you to visualize the portion of the world surrounding that emotion, and to prevent you from consistently visualizing the portion of the world in which you're trying to create an original idea. So if something is going on in your life that your mind just can't put aside—whether it's your family's upcoming vacation to Walt Disney World (usually, but not always, considered a positive thing) or the very expensive dent you just put into your bumper in the parking lot (definitely a negative)—asking yourself to ignore it is going to have no more effect than asking the rain to stop.

The science confirms this. As the discussion in that paper about arousal continues, it says, "Extremely high levels of arousal reduce the capacity to perceive, process and evaluate information."[7] Interestingly, this finding parallels very recent research on a highly related cognitive process, the exercise of willpower. As a 2009 scientific paper put it, "self-regulatory strength is a finite, renewable resource that is drained when people attempt to regulate their emotions, thoughts or behaviors."[8]

Unfortunately, science offers no prescriptions here to help you in the immediate term, at least with respect to creativity. (In the case of willpower, it dances around the issue, but effectively says, "Just go ahead and eat the cake—save your willpower for the more important stuff." We're not kidding; you can look it up for yourself.[9]) From our own experience, though, we can suggest one prescription to help you in the immediate term. Learn which kinds of emotional overhead you personally are capable of temporarily ignoring, and which ones you are not. Ask yourself which types of distractions prey on your emotions. Which are merely annoyances and which cause total shutdown? Knowing the difference will enable you to proceed when you might have thought you couldn't, and to avoid the frustration of certain failure by not even attempting to be creative at a time when it simply wouldn't work.

Thankfully, both science and our experience do provide more help in the medium term: you can build up your ability to neutralize emotional overhead over time. As the author of that paper on willpower put it, "You can actually increase your self-regulatory capacity. Willpower is like a muscle: it needs to be challenged to build itself."[10]

In our experience, this is best done first by learning to compartmentalize your mind so that when you're on the job creatively, fewer and fewer factors can overwhelm your emotions. It just takes practice. Begin with low-level mental tasks at first, then work your way up to high-level tasks (such as creating new ideas) over the course of a few weeks.

We both learned this valuable life lesson when we sold books door to door during summers in college. Believe it or not, selling those books was probably one of the most valuable jobs—and certainly the most emotionally difficult job—either of us has ever held. The job actually requires a fair amount of creativity to overcome the myriad problems you face (like getting arrested on your first day in the field for going door to door without the license we'd been told we didn't need; after one great sales demonstration on the hood of the cop's patrol car, we were free to go). But far more important than creativity, the job requires you to control your emotions in order to be effective.

Here's what happens. The company sends you to some small town you've never heard of, so that you have no friends to distract you from working the "strongly recommended" eighty hours per week (no, we're not kidding—that's the standard, and believe it or not, most of their salespeople observe it). Six days a week, from 8:00 a.m. until as late as 10:00 p.m., you go door to door. Some potential customers are rude, some openly hostile. You're supposed to demonstrate your product thirty times a day—but that may mean knocking on sixty or more doors, because many people, understandably, won't even let you in their home. Furthermore, if you succeed in doing your thirty demos, you will on average be told no twenty-seven times. A few noes come quickly and cleanly, but most of the people to whom you give your demonstration are too polite to give you a direct rejection (remember, these are the ones who were kind enough to let you in the door). So they inadvertently string you along, getting your hopes up, before finally saying no.

To say the least, the job gets to you emotionally at certain times. To get a sense of what it's like, imagine this demonstration the company used to conduct in front of hundreds of rookie salespeople during week one of sales training each summer.

A trainer blows up thirty large balloons, then stands behind a door with the balloons and a pin. You knock on the door. The trainer/mock customer opens the door, takes one look at you, then either slams the door in your face (half the time), or hands you a balloon (half the time). If he hands you the balloon, you hold it up and start talking.

As you talk, the trainer suddenly sticks the pin in the balloon so it blows up in your face. This sequence of events is then repeated twenty-nine times, with the next balloon potentially exploding at any time. During the course of the demonstration, the trainer can, at his sole discretion, let one, two, or three random balloons survive until the end of your talk—but no more than three. The others all get blown up in your face.

That's like one day on the job. Now imagine doing it every day, six days a week, for ten weeks, in a town full of strangers located somewhere in rural Kentucky or Mississippi. Feeling pretty good so far?

Here's the rub: In order to succeed at this job, *you must present a bright, confident, and friendly face at every door.* Otherwise, you'll sell nothing—as we can personally attest. The trick is, you must learn to compartmentalize your mind. Mrs. Jones at the next door doesn't know or care that the last customer was rude (happened perhaps a thousand times). She doesn't know that you haven't sold a single book all day (happened dozens of times). She doesn't know that your girlfriend just dumped you because you've been too busy to write to her all summer (happened, but thankfully only once). The only person who can bring all that baggage to the next door is you—and if you bring it, you won't make a sale. So you learn to recognize which baggage is irrelevant to your next task—and leave it behind.

Fortunately for you, it's not necessary to sell books door to door to learn how to compartmentalize your thinking. (And, by the way, don't feel sorry for us. In the interests of full disclosure, we should tell you that you can learn—and earn—a lot more by selling books door to door than by lifeguarding for the summer.) You can learn to do it simply by practicing any time you experience an emotional event in your life and yet are forced by circumstances to concentrate on an important mental task. Soon you'll learn that you can perform low-level tasks without becoming overwhelmed. Then move on to higher level ones. Finally you'll develop enough control to perform even challenging creative tasks—even if you're leaving tomorrow morning on that trip to visit Mickey Mouse.

UNDERSTANDING YOUR PERSONAL RESPONSE TO INTRINSIC AND EXTRINSIC MOTIVATIONS

It seems to go without saying that motivation is essential for the creative process. Therefore, you might reasonably conclude that motivation of any kind is good, and more is better.

However, such reasonable thinking can be wrong. In her 2003 article "The Social Psychology of Creativity," prominent psychologist Beth Hennessey wrote, "Researchers and theorists now understand that there is a direct relation between the motivational orientation brought to a task and the likelihood of creativity at that task."[11] She then went on to distinguish between intrinsic motivation and extrinsic motivation. Intrinsic motivation refers to self-motivation, and it stems from sources like curiosity about the subject at hand, enjoyment of the task itself, feelings of competence or mastery, sense of control, and so on. Extrinsic motivation refers to external stimuli such as economic or social rewards, evaluation, deadlines, competition, and supervision.

Why is this distinction so important? Because the first twenty-five years of motivational research that recognized this distinction produced a stark conclusion: intrinsic motivation *improved* creativity, while extrinsic motivation *impeded* creativity. (In fact, a crude, over-simplified version of this point of view led to widespread teaching of an absurd approach to managing creative people, one that we'll explore in Chapter 8.)

Since then, researchers have discovered many nuances, exceptions, and conditions that affect their earlier, simplistic findings. But the net result is that there are important differences in how the two kinds of motivation affect people in general, and important variations in how each of them affects different people individually. And since both kinds of motivation are present in almost any idea-creation setting, it's important for you to understand how your individual creativity is affected by intrinsic and extrinsic motivators.

For example, research shows that the promise of a reward based on task completion (an extrinsic motivator) usually undermines both intrinsic motivation and creativity. (In short, in the presence of a reward for getting the task done, many people lose interest in getting it done creatively.) It's as if people feel a fixed amount of total motivation, and external motivation simply pushes out internal motivation. But that's not true for all circumstances or for all people. For some people, the reward simply feels like a bonus—in addition to whatever intrinsic motivators they were feeling—and their creativity actually increases.

Other extrinsic motivations have even more complex impacts. For example, when faced with the knowledge that their performance will be evaluated (an extrinsic motivator), the creativity of shy people seems to fall significantly—but this is generally not the case for people who are *not* shy. Another example: boys tend to demonstrate more creativity under competitive conditions, but girls tend to demonstrate less. And another: a study of computer science students showed that low-skill students wrote more creative programs when expecting an evaluation, but higher skill students wrote less creative ones under the same conditions.

Sometimes the impact of extrinsic motivators seemed to be purely a function of people's attitudes. In a study of commissioned and non-commissioned works done by professional artists (that is, works for which the artist agreed up front to produce a certain work for a fee versus works that the artist created spontaneously of his or her own accord), attitudes of the artists toward the commission varied widely. Those who saw it as a controlling constraint produced works that were far less creative than their norm. On the other hand, those who looked on the commission as a confirmation of their competence by respected observers produced works that were more creative than their norm.

The driving factors are many and complex, but the practical conclusion for you is simple and straightforward. The variance in thought processes among individuals is very wide. Therefore, you need to develop your own personal understanding of how intrinsic and extrinsic factors affect your creativity—not how they affect any demographic subgroup on average—and act accordingly. With that personal understanding in hand, you can work to alter the conditions that surround your ideation sessions, increasing positive factors and avoiding negative factors.

In the real world, you don't have complete control over the presence of extrinsic motivators, even if some of them impede your personal creativity. There are (and as we'll argue in Chapter 8, there *should* be) deadlines, evaluations, monetary consequences, and so on, whether you like it or not. Fortunately, social psychologists have developed the beginnings of an approach that can help you mitigate their negative impact. In a series of studies, Hennessey and her colleagues showed that if you take time (prior to beginning the creative task itself) to focus on and reinforce the intrinsic motivation aspects of the task (such as remembering the inherently interesting, fun, and playful aspects of the task), then look for ways to enhance those aspects and psychologically distance yourself from any negative extrinsic aspects of the task, you'll be more creative.[12]

TAILORING THE IDEA-GENERATION PROCESS TO YOUR PERSONAL STYLE

Much has been written over the years regarding "the best" process to maximize your creativity, involving tailoring the physical environment, conducting physical and mental exercises, and so on. Much of that material is junk.

Physical environment? We've seen great ideas emerge from soulless conference rooms and from anonymous desks in the middle of cubicle farms. We've seen useless ideas come out of those "cool" office spaces that the dot-coms once craved. Physical and mental exercises to warm up your mind? Our personal favorite was the ideation guru who forced his clients to wear paper diapers on their heads and run around Lower Manhattan in order to open up their minds to the creative process. (Aren't you glad that you bought this book instead of his?)

The primary problem with this entire body of thought is that it attempts to establish a single set of process rules for everyone to follow. Don't get us wrong—we do believe there are times when rules help, particularly when people are trying to invent ideas in groups. In those situations (which we'll explore in the next chapter), certain rules can help you organize the process to effectively leverage a number of common psychological patterns in the way people work together in collective problem-solving situations. But individual idea creation is different. The variance in thought processes used by individuals is actually much wider than the variance in thought processes used by groups. So instead of following a single, universal prescription, you should do whatever makes *you* most effective.

That doesn't mean you should do just anything. It means you should devote some mental energy to learning what choices make you most effective. For starters, you need to know where your personal optimum point lies in four aspects of your idea-generation process: length of sessions; time between sessions; the role (if any) of a sounding board; and reusing the same questions.

Length of Sessions

The time you devote to a single idea-generation session should be based solely on how long you, personally, can stay focused on a particular problem without wandering off topic.

Your ability to stay focused will be affected by the structure of the task itself. For example, after the first exercise in Chapter 1 (the one in which we gave you the completely unstructured task of inventing a new business), we mentioned that most people give up after less than five minutes. In fact, that's typical for highly unstructured tasks—the very lack of structure leads the mind to wander.

When we gave you the additional structure of the "emotionally powerful as a child/expensive form for adults" question, you probably found that you could go for fifteen minutes before losing concentration. Again that's typical. And when we ran you through the perfect gift exercise at the end of Chapter 3, we suggested you allot about thirty minutes to work through three different questions. With the additional structure provided by having to refocus every ten minutes, most people find that they can keep going, all by themselves, for the full thirty minutes. (In the next chapter, we'll see how changing from an individual working alone to a small group of people working together can successfully extend people's ideation intervals even further.)

But in addition to varying with the structure of the task, all these time intervals can vary significantly by individual. What exactly was your experience with the three exercises? Did you find that you gave up more quickly than most people, or that you were still going strong at the end and only your stopwatch prevented you from working longer? When you were looking for the perfect gift, did you add a fourth question? Analyze these patterns to begin understanding your own personal comfort zone.

For example, the two of us work very differently from each other. One of us is generally very calm and methodical, while the other is far more fidgety. The latter one usually thinks in high-intensity short bursts—unless he hits on a new insight that intrigues him, in which case he can wrestle with one question or insight for an unusually long time, well after other people have worn out. Over the years, we've learned to work (and work together) in ways that fit with these patterns. We don't try to force-fit one of our styles into the other, and we completely ignore any expert's dogmatic views regarding any single "right" time intervals.

Time Between Sessions

How quickly should you move from one Right Question (or idea) to the next? Should you do it right away, or take a break? That depends on how long it takes you to let go of the ideas you generated using one question before you can take a truly fresh perspective using a second question. For some people, this mental task of switching channels comes easily. Others can remain wrapped up in—or even haunted by—their previous thoughts, and therefore need a break between idea-generation episodes.

If you occasionally fall into the latter camp, that's A-OK. We find that when people can't get a certain idea out of their minds, there's usually some unresolved issue about it that prevents them from letting it rest. They use phrases like "It's just not quite right yet," or "There's something wrong, I just can't put my finger on it yet." That's perfectly fine—stay with the old question until you can let it go. Since in this chapter, you're still working alone, you needn't feel bound by any time limits.

On the other hand, if this is a chronic problem for you, even after taking breaks, you may need to interfere with your own tendency. Otherwise, the only question you'll gain full value from during any Brainsteering exercise will be the first one you ask. And since, as we saw in Chapter 2, there's no way to know in advance which question will be the absolute "best" question, you need to be at full strength for every question.

Fortunately, the solution is simple once you realize that you need it. You should select the full set of questions you intend to use in any one particular session before you jump into answering any of them. Then arrange the questions in a sequence that maximizes the disparity of the perspectives taken as you move from question to question. For example, pretend you want to search for the perfect gift by using three questions from the list we gave you at the end of Chapter 3—say, questions 1 and 3 from the heartwarming list, and question 3 from the giver-centric list. Logically, you might plan to ask yourself the questions in just that order—but that would be a mistake. It's likely that there's a high degree of overlap between the favorite period of your loved one's life and the people that he or she was once close to. Therefore, you should position the giver-centric question in between the other two. That will force your mind away from your intended recipient's past. Then when you begin thinking of people he or she was close to in the past, you'll have an easier time thinking of additional people besides those who happened to be associated with that one favorite period.

Role of a Sounding Board

Do you remember that old saying, which was meant to encourage listening to others, about how "you can never learn anything if you do all the talking"? It's well intentioned—but it's wrong.

Sometimes the mere act of articulating your ideas can help you improve them. Explaining an idea to someone else forces you to be specific, to spell out your assumptions, to hammer out inconsistencies, and to adjust the idea in order to overcome skepticism. Therefore, consider finding someone to act as your sounding board.

Note that this is *not* the same as having an idea development partner; that's a different role. A person playing the role of sounding board does almost nothing but listen, reflect your own idea back to you, and ask questions if he doesn't understand the concept or follow your logic. (In fact, if a sounding board tries too hard, he can actually reduce your effectiveness.) He doesn't have to be your intellectual equal, doesn't need to have your years of training and experience, doesn't need to complement your skill set, and may not even need to understand all of the considerations and constraints that shape your thinking. Your newest employee can often make a good sounding board. It's a relatively passive but very helpful role. Ask yourself: Who can play that valuable role for you?

Reusing the Same Questions

As we showed in Chapter 4, even creative people can fall into the rut of using the same questions over and over if they're not careful. We also showed you how you can avoid such a rut. But does that mean you should never reuse a question that's proved successful for you in the past? Not at all. We've used some of our favorite questions dozens of times in many different client settings (tailored to the specific application, of course, and often with different signpost examples).

How long must you wait before reusing the same question? As always, that's for you to decide—but there is one very specific criterion for making that decision. You should return to a previously successful question only when enough time has passed for your new ideas to be something other than minor variants of the ideas you thought of last time. Only you can know exactly when that is, but you can easily monitor yourself. Try repeating your most successful question the next time you need an idea. If the ideas it generates are distinctly different from the previous set, great. If not, put the question away for longer and longer periods until it truly becomes a fresh question again.

HANDLING THE "IDEA REQUEST FROM HELL"

At some point, particularly if you develop a reputation for developing good ideas, you're going to be put on the spot with what we'll call the "idea request from hell." The request will be for an idea that falls right in the center of your weak spot. The requestor will be someone important, like your boss—and your idea will be needed within a much shorter time frame than you normally spend developing your best ideas. Oh, yeah—and the request will come at a time when you're emotionally overloaded to begin with.

Don't panic. Remember that ancient saying: "In the land of the blind, the one-eyed man is king." The requestor apparently has zero good ideas to work with at this point, or else he wouldn't be standing in front of you in such a time crunch. So you probably don't have to generate the best idea of your life here. Any reasonably good idea will be a gift, something better than whatever he's got right now: nada.

Take a deep breath. Then look at the person standing in front of you and decide instantly which of two types of requestor he is.

Type 1: The Thought Partner. He genuinely needs, and wants, a good idea, and he's come to seek your help in finding one. And fortunately, he constitutes the majority of the population.

If your requestor is a Thought Partner, revert to your short list of "ace in the hole" Right Questions—the ones that have accounted for most of your best ideas as you've built your reputation—or consult the appendix of this book, where you'll find a handy list of 101 Right Questions to stimulate breakthrough ideas. (Suddenly, you're *really* glad that you bought this book.) Your favorite Right Questions—even ones you've temporarily retired because your ideas were getting more pedestrian—will get you off to a productive start.

Think out loud, opening with a recitation of one of your all-time favorites. The requestor will be impressed with your list of questions that immediately start generating possibilities. More than likely, he'll even participate in generating new ideas with you, bouncing ideas back and forth. He'll credit you with helping, even if he's the one who actually originates the Reasonably Good Idea. The two of you will succeed together.

Type 2: Mr. Why Don't You Yes But, or WDYYB for short. He should be approached with much more caution. You've met this guy at various times throughout your life, and he's an expert at a psychological game first made famous way back in 1964 by psychiatrist Eric Berne in his best-selling book *Games People Play: The Psychology of Human Relationships.* Berne's book has sold over five million copies by describing, in layman's terms, a host of functional and dysfunctional social interactions.[13]

The concept of this game can be instantly understood when you see how its name reads using conversational punctuation, as in: "Why don't you . . . ?" "Yes, but . . . " In WDYYB, one person poses a problem that he cannot solve, ostensibly asking for the listener's help. However, every idea that the listener suggests will be greeted with some reason why that idea won't work. The real motivation of the first person is *not* to find a solution to the problem, but to justify why he can't solve it by "proving" that the second person can't find a solution either.

Of course, there are many real barriers that can prevent ideas being successful, and the requestor's rejection of your initial ideas might be legitimate. But you've probably had experience with this person before, so hopefully you'll already have a sense as to whether you're dealing with a legitimate Type 1 Thought Partner who just happened to spot a flaw in your first idea, or a scurrilous Type 2 Mr. WDYYB. (And be warned: according to Berne, the "victim" can never win this game, no matter how good their suggestions. Berne says the only solution is to refuse to play the game. That's fine—unless the requestor is your boss.)

If you determine that you're dealing with Mr. WDYYB, here's what you do to give yourself at least a fighting chance. First ask him, "What's the idea you're going to go with if we can't come up with a better one?" That will establish an explicit benchmark—your idea doesn't have to be perfect, just better than the current one. Then ask him, "What's the main problem with that idea?" because (remember the value of constraining your lines of thinking from Chapter 1?) your single highest probability of success will lie with finding ways to deal with the existing problems of the current idea, not a brand-new idea. In addition, this question will flush out the most likely objections that Mr. WDYYB will have to your own ideas, and prevent you from suggesting any ideas that fall into the same trap.

If you need to continue, revert to your "ace in the hole" Right Questions—but in this case, do *not* think out loud. You'll recall from Chapter 1 that the first iteration of any idea is usually not very good. Therefore, don't give Mr. WDYYB a cheap shot at a fragile idea—because once he rejects an idea, he probably won't respond to any incremental improvements.

Once you've identified two or three possibilities, tell the requestor to lower his expectations before you describe your ideas out loud, as in, "Given the short time frame we're facing here, I'm not sure I can come up with a *perfect* solution, but let's try these on for size, because they may be better than our current alternative." That way, the psychology of the requestor is preserved without having to bring down your ideas. And don't forget to present your ideas with an open invitation for him to improve upon them. You might even mention a possible drawback or two that he can solve. You may not succeed every time, but if his psychological malady is mild, you might just come up with something that makes him—and you—look good.

PART III

LEAD OTHERS TO GREAT IDEAS

7

From a Bad Brainstorming Session to a Great Brainsteering Workshop

We've all experienced it. A bunch of people, chosen largely for political reasons, show up in a big conference room. Standing at the front of the room is a professional "creativity moderator," who doesn't understand the nature of your company's business—and doesn't think he should have to. He admonishes the group, "Get creative! Think outside the box!" But many attendees remain true to their ingoing promise to themselves that they would not say a word throughout the day. As a result, three pushy people (who, unfortunately, did not make the same promise to themselves) dominate the session with their pet ideas. Ideas pop up randomly in all directions. And since the moderator cheerily instructed everyone at the outset, "There are no bad ideas!" a lot of airtime and energy gets taken up by preposterous ideas. Further, because the session has no structure, no momentum ever builds around improving, or creating variants of, the best ideas. And finally, because "it's impossible to mandate the production of good ideas," most attendees think it's okay to produce nothing—which is exactly what the session does. As the group trundles out of the room at 5:00 p.m., various people can be heard whispering,

"Another wasted day . . . when do I get to do my *real* work? . . . Nothing's going to come out of this session either."

Sound harsh? Or painfully familiar? If you're like most people, you've experienced it firsthand many times. And unfortunately, you're not alone—bad brainstorming sessions are actually the norm, not the exception.

That's right: the most widely utilized group ideation technique in the world usually fails. As we detailed in the introduction, when Alex Osborn first promoted the technique of brainstorming in the 1950s, he claimed that brainstorming would enable a group to produce both a greater quantity and a greater quality of ideas than could be produced by individuals working alone. But when numerous academic researchers empirically tested those assertions in a variety of studies over the following decades, they found that the exact opposite is true. The studies consistently showed that rather than follow the traditional brainstorming approach, a leader would be better off to simply gather the team together, inform them of the ideation goals to be pursued, and then send each team member off to a separate room to work alone for the same length of time that he or she would have spent in the group session.

So should you simply reject group problem solving?

Not at all. While some tasks should be undertaken alone, there are clear advantages to people working together. Each person possesses different information and experience, and it may well be that one person's information and experience will enable a second person to think of an idea that the first person would never have found. In addition, one person's ideas will often cause a second person to think up a different idea, or an improved version of the first idea.

But if you're going to be leading any kind of group ideation exercise, you should make sure you do it the right way.

As we mentioned in the introduction, the problem with traditional brainstorming is that its methodology violates many of the psychological and sociological principles regarding how human beings work best together in a group setting. Researchers have consistently seen this and have extensively described a number of the key problem factors—and success factors—over the years. We've used those factors to develop a better process: the Brainsteering version of the group ideation process.

Before we begin, we must warn you that organizing a great Brainsteering workshop will require more mental effort and preparation on your part than a traditional brainstorming session—but we can guarantee you that your extra work will be worth the trouble.

THE COST OF BAD BRAINSTORMING

Have you ever paused to calculate the true cost of a typical corporate brainstorming session?

First, there are the direct costs. Suppose twenty people spend a full day off-site with a facilitator. The salary and benefits cost of the attendees probably totals over $8,000 (twenty people, whose average compensation is $75,000 plus benefits, each of whom works about 230 days a year). Then there are the room and food costs (perhaps $500), and the facilitator's fee (usually $1,000 or more—sometimes much more). By the time you factor in planning time and administrative support, not to mention any travel costs, it's easy to reach a total of $10,000 or more.

Then you've got the indirect costs. What else could those people have been doing? If this session produces only mediocre ideas, what's the opportunity cost of not pursuing the better ideas that might have emerged from a more successful one? And speaking of mediocre ideas, how much cost might the company incur when, having spent a substantial sum to hold the session in the first place, it then feels compelled to implement one or more of the mediocre ideas that come out of it? Or what if the company actually does *nothing* substantial after the session to follow up—like most companies that hold traditional brainstorming sessions? Isn't that equally bad? In any event, an unproductive brainstorming session clearly produces a variety of burdens on the company that go far beyond its direct costs.

The same phenomenon is true for smaller efforts too, of course. If you're planning a fund-raiser for your favorite charity, the direct costs of your session may be lower, but the opportunity costs are likely to be every bit as high, because you'll probably feel compelled to implement whatever idea emerges from the group session, even if it's only mediocre.

No matter what context you happen to be working in, there's clearly a lot at stake in any group ideation exercise. So if you plan to conduct one, it's worth investing whatever extra time and effort might be required to do it right.

THE ANSWER, IN A NUTSHELL

In the following pages, we'll explore all the key principles and techniques that will enable you turn a bad brainstorming session into a great Brainsteering workshop. But to get you started, here's a one-paragraph summary.

In a Brainsteering workshop, you break up the usual group of ten to twenty participants into subgroups composed of three to five people each. Each subgroup focuses on developing ideas using a single question that you assign, and sticks with that task for thirty to forty-five minutes. Each subgroup then moves on to another question for a similar period, and so on, for five or six rounds—at which point they're typically exhausted but very excited about several of the ideas they've developed. At the end of the day, each subgroup removes any weak ideas from its list. Beyond that, the combined group of attendees does *not* make any effort to select the best ideas of the day. Instead, immediately after the session, you as the moderator meet with a subset of key managers and force real decisions to be made about what actions will actually be taken, and you make certain to promptly communicate those decisions (whether good news or bad) back to the workshop participants.

Seems pretty easy, doesn't it? In many ways it is. Although the science behind the design is quite sophisticated—and although, as you'll see below, there are several additional details you'll have to manage very carefully—the basic process of conducting a Brainsteering workshop is straightforward enough that virtually anyone who's willing to put in the work can organize a successful one.

BEFORE THE WORKSHOP

A great Brainsteering workshop begins with careful planning, much more careful planning than most people are used to. In fact, about 80 percent of the additional investment of time and effort that we warned you about occurs here, in conducting four sets of tasks.

Understand the real criteria that will be used to make decisions about the workshop's ideas. How many times have you learned, after the fact, that the best ideas to come out of a brainstorming session were actually dead on arrival? That they lay beyond anything your organization was willing to remotely consider? Frustrating, wasn't it?

In our view, such occasions are a failure of both the traditional brainstorming methodology and the session leader. "Think outside the box!" is not a helpful exhortation if external circumstances or some important policies create a box that the organization *must* live within. And why didn't the session leader tell the participants where the limits were?

So start by finding out and articulating the real criteria that will be used to make decisions about the ideas that may come out of your workshop. First, *are there any absolute constraints?* For example, we once participated in an old-fashioned brainstorming session at a bank in which the entire session was rendered moot because all of the better ideas required changes to the company's IT systems, and the bank—without ever informing any of the participants in the session—had recently declared that its IT agenda was "locked down" for the next eighteen months.

Next, *what constitutes an acceptable idea?* For example, in working with a (different, smarter) bank to develop growth ideas, we helped top management guide the business units as follows: "For this particular workshop, we want practical, affordable, short-term ideas. A great idea will be one that requires no more than $5,000 per branch in investment (capital or expense), and generates incremental profits within twelve months. Furthermore, while we are willing to consider new product ideas, sales approaches, and pricing, we are not willing to seek any new regulatory approvals."

Finally, *how will one acceptable idea be chosen over another?* For example, is upside potential more important than downside risk, or vice versa? (This will influence all of your subsequent decisions.) Is it better for solutions to fit easily within the existing way of doing things, or does the decision maker want to "shake things up" or "really make a splash"? What expectations might there be about the time frame to implementation, or about payback?

Select the right questions. Throughout this book, we've emphasized the importance of finding and using Right Questions. Now comes your best chance ever to put that advice into action. Remember from Chapter 2 that for any given application, all questions are not created equal—some are better for today's purpose, others for tomorrow's.

First, select from your arsenal the best candidate questions you can find, until you have the same number of questions as you have "subgroup ideation sessions" (as detailed below, sessions in which subgroups of three to five people spend thirty to forty-five minutes focusing on a single question).

Then arrange those questions in order from "best" (for today's purpose only) to "worst," keeping in mind that a wonderful question might get graded lower in this particular instance if it adopts a similar perspective to another question that's already higher on your list.

Next, ask yourself whether you believe that there is a higher likelihood of a great idea emerging from (1) having any subgroups work with the "worst" question from the ones you selected, versus (2) having multiple subgroups work with your single "best" question. If the answer is (2), then drop your "worst" question and have two subgroups use the "best" question. Keep asking yourself this question—recognizing that each time you assign the same question to an additional group, they will come up with a certain number of different ideas but progressively more duplicate ideas—until you feel like you've achieved the optimum balance.

Finally, don't forget to tailor the questions as we discussed in Chapter 3.

Choose the right people. The golden rule for selecting participants for your Brainsteering workshop is deceptively straightforward: pick people who can answer the questions you plan to ask, and who have the mental orientation to translate those answers into ideas.

However, as obvious as this rule sounds, it's actually telling you to do something very different from what most leaders of traditional brainstorming do. Most leaders tend to choose the attendees first, without regard to their specific knowledge. Further, they tend to use stale formulas when deciding whom to invite, as in "We have to invite Fred—after all, he *is* the head of marketing."

A couple of years ago, we worked with a large catalog retailer that sold many of its items on credit. The company accepted ordinary credit cards like Visa and MasterCard, but it was also willing to extend credit directly to customers who, for whatever reason, preferred not to use an ordinary credit card. Of course, this meant that just like the ordinary credit card companies, the retailer frequently had problems collecting on bad debts. We were asked to run a Brainsteering workshop on improving bad debt collections.

One subgroup was discussing the Right Question "What has changed in our operating environment since we last redesigned our processes?" when, about halfway through the designated thirty-minute time frame for that question, a longtime frontline collections manager announced: "Well, death has become the new bankruptcy."

A few other managers laughed knowingly, but the rest of us—including several senior executives of the company—didn't get the joke. "Well," he explained, "when I first started working here, people used to get us to stop calling them by telling us that they had declared bankruptcy—because, of course, you can't cost-effectively collect loans for our relatively inexpensive products after a bankruptcy. We eventually learned that many of them were simply lying, so we started requiring documentation, and the false claims of bankruptcy dropped dramatically. But now, borrowers who want to stiff us simply get someone else in the household to tell us that they've died. We often know the person on the phone is lying to us, particularly if this isn't the first time we've called the house. (A lot of times, we'd love to ask, 'Oh, did you forget that last week you told me he couldn't come to the phone because he was still at work?' but of course we can't.) The thing is, they know we're not going to be so impolite as to demand a death certificate—so 'death' has become the new 'bankruptcy'!"

While this wasn't the largest problem the collectors faced, it still represented a significant opportunity—and none of the senior executives had heard about this spreading practice. We learned of it only by having frontline managers in the workshop.

Interestingly, while that manager identified the opportunity, he wasn't the person who provided the idea needed to capture the opportunity. That idea came from another frontline manager, who said: "We can't be so impolite as to demand a death certificate, but we *could* tell them—truthfully—that we're required by the company to document all write-offs for our records. 'So, Mrs. Jones, would you wait for just a minute while I double-check the tape recorder, then state for the record your name, address, relationship to the deceased, and state, also for the record, when the person died?' Many people are willing to casually lie for someone else—but few are willing to provide 'smoking gun' evidence of fraud."

So a good idea emerged as the result of two smart choices about attendees, not just one.

Separate attendees into small subgroups and match the questions to the subgroups. As we've discussed, a single combined brainstorming session with a large group of people simply doesn't work. Instead, split the attendees into subgroups of three to five people.

Why at least three? Because two people don't bring enough different perspectives to really "mix things up." And because when two people are paired up, one person usually dominates the other in conversation, but that's much less likely to happen when there are three, four, or five people in the subgroup.

Five or fewer people constitute a small subgroup. Why no more than five? Because in subgroups of no more than five people, the social dynamics reinforce the goal of the workshop instead of working against it. In Chapter 1, we saw that the social norm in a large group is to keep quiet. But just the opposite is true in a small subgroup—the social norm is to speak up. No one can hide, no one can fail to contribute without appearing to be a slacker, and no two people can drift off into an irrelevant side conversation without appearing rude to the other subgroup members. Once a subgroup has six or more members, all of these positive dynamics begin to slip away, and a noticeable decline in productivity follows.

Importantly, in assigning specific members to each subgroup, be sure to quarantine the "Idea Crushers." Idea Crushers are people who, intentionally or unintentionally, prevent others from putting forth good ideas. They come in three varieties: the Boss, the Big Mouth, and the Subject Matter Expert.

The presence of the Boss creates problems per se, because many people will be afraid to risk expressing an unproven idea in front of her. No matter how nice she is or how unthreatening her manner, the mere existence of her title will cause some people to go silent. This can be a particularly important issue if your workshop includes several levels of organization. ("Speak up in front of my boss's boss's boss? No, thank you.")

The Big Mouth takes up airtime, intimidates the less confident, and gives everyone else an excuse to be lazy. ("I don't have to come up with an idea—and I couldn't get a word in edgewise, anyway.")

The Subject Matter Expert crushes ideas, intentionally or unintentionally, because everyone defers to his superior knowledge—even if that knowledge is incomplete with regard to the particular issue at hand, or biased by his own unrepresentative experiences. Further, we often find that the more expert a person is in the way things are *currently* done, the less open-minded he is about how they *could be* done better.

That's right. In complete contrast to that old brainstorming adage about mixing all types of people together in any session, we're telling you to isolate the Idea Crushers in a single subgroup. If you spread them around, they'll crush all your subgroups, but if you put them in group quarantine, the other subgroups will be free to think creatively. (And by the way—you won't be wasting the time of the Idea Crushers. In our experience, their subgroup will produce ideas, too, because Idea Crushers rarely stop *each other* from speaking up.)

With the design of your subgroups in hand, you can then assign specific questions to each subgroup. You've probably already guessed how to do that: each subgroup should be assigned the questions that they are best positioned to answer. And if there's a question that you especially like, but no particular subgroup has quite the right knowledge to answer it, assign it to whichever group contains the Big Mouths. It will never even occur to them that they don't have enough knowledge to answer it. (Oh, come on. We're not being mean. You know that's *exactly* how Big Mouths think.)

RUNNING THE WORKSHOP ITSELF

Most of the time in a Brainsteering workshop will be spent with the subgroups working separately. But first you have to orient everyone collectively. Then the subgroups will need to follow a specific process. And finally, you'll need to conclude the workshop on a constructive note that's *not* the one you'd expect.

Orient the participants. Remember that your participants are probably expecting a typical brainstorming session. So at the outset of your workshop, you must take them on a brief intellectual journey, a miniature version of the one you've traveled in this book.

First, they must come to believe that a question-based approach can help generate ideas at all. Then they must come to believe that a question-based approach can lead to ideas that meet their particular challenge. Your group may need you to demonstrate a question in a context that's similar to their task, complete with signpost examples. When doing so, it's best to show them an example from an analogous—but not identical—setting. That way, they can see the analogy, but they won't get defensive about whether the specific example ideas would work in their setting.

Next, transition from teaching the overall Brainsteering approach to describing the goals of the day. Your participants need to understand the specific goals of the workshop, the criteria for creating new ideas, and any constraints the ideas must fit within, all of which you developed earlier.

Then describe the participants' roles. Explain that their work will be conducted in preassigned subgroups, that the day will consist of a series of x-minute ideation sessions in which their subgroup will be given a single question to answer.

And—very important—set their expectations appropriately by explaining to them that each of their individual ideation sessions will likely produce only two or three worthy ideas. Remember how we warned you in the perfect gift exercise to expect only two to four ideas from each question? We did that so that you would have realistic expectations, to make sure you didn't become discouraged and quit too soon. Here, the danger is even greater. For most people, getting just two or three ideas from the combined effort of three to five people over the course of twenty, or thirty, or forty-five minutes *feels* like failure. But as we'll see below, it's most definitely not failure; it's actually a huge success. So your participants need to know what constitutes success, and recognize that along the way, success can feel like pretty slow going.

Finish your intro with a parlor trick. If you want to boost the energy level of the group just as they turn to looking for ideas—and hey, who wouldn't want to do that?—take this lesson from our time in the trenches: parlor tricks work, even when you'd think they wouldn't.

We once held a Brainsteering workshop with the top eight executives of one of America's ten largest corporations. Each of these guys (yes, unfortunately, even in this day and age, the top eight executives were all "guys") made over $3 million a year and held stock worth many millions more. Each was a gruff executive who had started in a manufacturing plant and clawed his way through the bureaucracy to the top. Somehow we cajoled each man to put $20 into a pot, with the pot to be awarded to the executive who developed the single best idea, to be judged at the end of the day by simple vote among the eight. It worked. They were all over their assignments like paparazzi on Britney Spears. Winning that pool of $160 meant more to them than the actual value of the ideas to their multibillion company and the subsequent boost to their own net worth.

There are lots of parlor tricks available, but look for one that your audience has never seen before. You could announce at the outset of the workshop that the originator(s) of any big new product idea will have their initials hidden somewhere on the packaging of that product. Let the winner appear as an extra in the background of a television commercial. Hold up an autographed photo of Elvis—an allegedly genuine one is available on eBay at the time of this writing for $89.97—and promise it to the originator of whichever idea is later chosen by the workshop's sponsor as the best idea. (Note: this last parlor trick works best in small Southern cities, Las Vegas, and Branson, Missouri.)

Conduct each ideation session according to a strict formula. After the parlor trick, break the group into the assigned subgroups. No trading places, no last-minute giving in to some bigwig who says "But I think it would be best for the executives to see a cross section of the subgroups." You can tell them that we said their presence will ruin a subgroup's contributions. (That's right, blame us. We don't mind. In fact, while you're at it, tell them we said they don't pay you enough.)

At the beginning of each individual ideation session—but not before—give each subgroup one question. Their task is to work for thirty to forty-five minutes (your choice) with *only that one question*, to come up with ideas.

No idea from any other source, no matter how good it might be, should be mentioned during the ideation session. Tell the participants that if anyone happens to think of a "silver bullet," she should just silently write it down and bring it up later.

Why the strict formula? One of the worst aspects of old-fashioned brainstorming is the tendency for participants to ricochet from one shallow (and poor) idea to the next. The group never takes the time, and never develops the focus, to take a shallow idea and mold it into a better one ("Hmmm, that wouldn't work everywhere, but under *these* circumstances . . . That would be too expensive, but if we changed *this* part . . . A potential variant of that might be . . ."). Refining an idea, and identifying new and better ideas, both take time and focus.

By forcing each subgroup to stay with one question for thirty to forty-five minutes, you gain that time and focus. The first five minutes of any individual ideation session will sound like a typical brainstorming session, as most people push their old pet ideas or rattle off a superficial list of new lousy ones. The next ten minutes will produce a variety of better (but still mediocre) ideas. But then, in those last fifteen to thirty minutes, sparks will start to fly and better ideas will emerge. It's only when people have this additional time, and are prohibited from wandering off topic, that you'll see these ideas—the best ideas—emerge.

After thirty to forty-five minutes, give them another question, and repeat.

WRAPPING UP THE WORKSHOP

A few paragraphs ago, we mentioned that a single ideation session within a single subgroup should produce two or three worthy ideas. That implies that a group of twenty people using this workshop design for one day can produce about fifty to sixty worthy ideas by the time they're finished.

But which ideas are the best ones? It may not be obvious. So the next step is for the group as a whole to pick the best ones, right? *No.* While you should have each subgroup narrow its own list to eliminate ideas that its members think are subpar in light of the complete list they produced that day, do *not* allow the group as a whole to make any final choices.

Why not? Well, remember the "emotionally powerful as a child/ expensive form for adults" exercise? We love the exercise, because it's a very valuable teaching tool and people find it fun, especially when we let them vote on a winner at the end. However, the voting component of the exercise has a flaw: it produces predictable results in large crowds. For example, if the majority of the crowd consists of males between the ages of eighteen and thirty-five, then the winning idea will almost always involve *blowing something up*. Winning ideas have included playing army with real U.S. Army surplus tanks; making your own fireworks; or pretending to be a member of a special ops team conducting all sorts of covert operations involving C-4 explosives. Teams have invented private parks where, for ever larger fees, you can dynamite a tent, a car, a mobile home, a full-size house, or an entire fort. Yep, sure enough, if the majority of the voting audience is young men, whichever subgroup suggests an activity that ends with a big bang almost inevitably wins. There's just something about testosterone and adrenaline that seems to overwhelm balanced consideration of the merits of any alternative proposals.

At first, we thought we could live with this isolated flaw. After all, dynamite was rarely a feature of the ideas proposed in the "real" portions of our Brainsteering workshops (even those on cost reduction). But it turns out that *any* idea, if given a catchy name and presented with enough flair, can draw the short-term attention of the crowd at the end of a long day, regardless of its true merit or lack thereof.

We've seen it happen in every type of organization and in workshops on every topic. Crowds don't always have an understanding of all the criteria and considerations that must go into choosing one idea over others for actual investment. So don't ask them to choose—not only is it not helpful, it's also demotivating when their vote later gets overruled by those who actually *do* have to consider the full set of decision factors.

Your goal for the attendees at the end of the workshop should be limited to eliminating any ideas that are clearly below the bar, and to ensuring that the team members leave feeling good about having made a significant contribution to the organization's success.

But don't try to achieve the latter goal simply by thanking them. That doesn't work. Here's why: How often have you walked out of the room at the end of a brainstorming session just knowing that the ideas you produced are destined to disappear into the ether? Didn't you find that completely frustrating? To avoid having your Brainsteering workshop participants experience that sinking feeling, take the last few minutes of your workshop to describe for everyone *exactly* what steps will be taken (preferably the next day, as we describe next) to make firm decisions about the ideas generated today, and what steps will be taken to communicate those decisions to the participants.

AFTER THE WORKSHOP

Having generated a plethora of candidate ideas during your workshop, it's time to choose the best ones and make real commitments to take action—after all, no idea is worth anything until it's acted upon. So make some decisions *now*. And ensure those decisions get communicated immediately.

In our experience, the probability of real action resulting from any ideation event declines quickly with time unless firm decisions are made right away. That doesn't mean making a hasty, uninformed, or insufficiently researched decision to go national with some new product idea that was only dreamed up hours before. But it does mean deciding, firmly and promptly, which ideas to pursue at whatever is the appropriate next level of action.

We always try to preschedule a meeting with the key decision makers for the very next day, while all ideas are still fresh in people's minds. For example, when we recently served a southeastern university, the president and provost scheduled a full staff meeting the next morning at eight o'clock, where they worked with their top lieutenants to sort ideas into four buckets: reject, move immediately to implementation planning, decide today to implement the idea at the next appropriate juncture (such as the beginning of the next academic year), or assign a person or group—right then and there—to research the idea further.

Last, but definitely not least, all decisions must be communicated to the workshop participants—*even the rejections*. Some people have questioned our insistence that even the rejections be communicated. They fear rejection will be demotivating to the proposers of those ideas. But our experience is actually the opposite. Participants desperately want to know that they've been heard, that their ideas have at least had their day in court. They've gotten so used to hearing nothing after a session that they usually appreciate hearing any feedback—even a rejection—as it means their ideas were treated with respect and given a hearing, whether or not they made the final cut. Further, if you can respectfully communicate *why* certain ideas were rejected, that information helps participants improve their thinking and produce better ideas next time—and they *will* participate next time, often more eagerly than ever. We promise.

8

Teaching Others to Develop Better Ideas

We recently worked with the editors of a multibillion-dollar group of magazines, editors who faced a difficult dilemma. Circulation was down due to the "Great Recession," and the editors were caught in a vise. On the one hand, their staffs had been cut in order to preserve the profitability of their magazines. But on the other hand, they were under greater pressure than ever to maintain the quality of their stories to preserve circulation as best as they could. "Enlightened" advisors had suggested that the solution to their problem was empowerment: "Just give the existing staff more freedom to invent more stories with less supervision!" they were told.

The editors were reluctant, to say the least. As one of them put it to us early on, "Are they kidding? In this tough economic environment, my job is on the line for the quality of every issue. I can't take the quality risk of simply turning over final responsibility for stories to someone who I didn't believe was ready *before* we reduced staffing levels—when we also had more quality-control staffing and other safeguards in place than we do now."

It's the quintessential management problem. We need the leverage of giving more responsibility to junior people because the workload simply exceeds what the senior staff members can accomplish by them-selves. But no one's going to give us a free pass if those people make mistakes—and you *know* they're going to make mistakes somewhere along the way.

We all learned the solution in Management 101: delegation. Teach those junior staffers how to perform tasks better, so mistakes won't happen as often. Then delegate to them enough of your responsibili-ties that you free up a portion of your time to correct whatever mis-takes they make. Problem solved . . . in theory. The reality, of course, is much more complicated, beginning with the question "Exactly how do I teach them?" While this is always a hard question, it's especially hard when what your team produces is new ideas.

Many people believe that creativity can't be taught. But we know it can. We also know, from extensive experience, that one of the advan-tages of the tools and techniques in this book is that they can be taught more quickly, more easily, and more successfully than many others you may have been exposed to in the past. So how can you teach others to become sources of new, high quality ideas? By following four steps:

Establish a baseline standard of success.
Teach them the Brainsteering process in manageable steps.
Delegate appropriately.
Overcome your reluctance to provide feedback.

ESTABLISHING A BASELINE STANDARD OF SUCCESS

The most common underlying cause of mistakes by junior staffers at-tempting to create new ideas is that they've been given no model from which to recognize whether their idea is good or bad.

When this happens, most staffers migrate toward "safe" ideas that are largely imitative of past successes. Meanwhile, a few make the op-posite mistake: they try too hard to "be original" and produce fright-ening outputs. Both groups develop a set of superstitious explanations for their success or failure, often believing it's simply rooted in office politics ("They always like Joe's ideas, because he's their pet"). That superstition then interferes with their ability to search for the real criteria and thereby discover how to deliver better ideas. Consequently, the seniors come to view the juniors negatively ("They're just not as bright as we were when we were coming up") and they begin to lose confidence in them ("I just can't predict what tasks they can and can't accomplish").

The traditional solution to this problem was the apprentice system, in which the trainee would observe the master for an extended period during which the apprentice performed only low-risk tasks. In today's world, we usually can't afford the time lag associated with such a process. Fortunately, however, the problem can be largely addressed with just a few hours of work on your part. It turns out that a little information can substitute for a lot of experience. You just need to teach your young charges what success looks like.

To illustrate, put yourself in the shoes of a friend of ours. As the executive in charge of news gathering at a local TV station, he was unhappy with the quality of his news team's "nonbreaking" stories—that is, all the stories about subjects other than today's car wrecks, violent crimes, house fires, natural disasters, or political developments. In a typical half-hour newscast, they fill the fifteen minutes that come after the breaking news reports and before the weather and sports reports. Usually, "nonbreaking" stories don't have to air right away, so they're often used to help train the more junior producers and reporters (because the station has time to reshoot or reedit a story if the first version is subpar).

Our friend's problem was exacerbated by the fact that his news team included many junior staffers who frequently developed story ideas that were considered by their bosses to be off the mark in one way or another. To alleviate this problem, we had his senior team create a set of clear guidelines for putting together a good story, using three simple steps. (For our purposes here, we'll examine just one category of "nonbreaking" stories: scientific and technological discoveries.)

First, the team drafted a document that defined and illustrated several key points. It began by articulating the basic value proposition of their station's news department: "Our purpose is to report 'viewer-relevant news'—that is, news that affects (or could affect) each and every viewer directly."

Next, the document clarified what subjects were considered on target and which were off limits. For example, the station wanted stories about tangible scientific and technological inventions, not about such abstract discoveries as new mathematical concepts, theoretical physics, and so on. Further, the invention had to have the potential to alleviate a problem that many viewers (or their friends or loved ones) might face today. It might be a breakthrough medical cure, or simply a new software program that would manage stoplights more effectively in urban areas and thereby ease traffic problems—just as long as a broad cross section of the audience could relate to it.

Next, the document spelled out criteria regarding the onscreen telling of the story. For example, the producer had to find an expert on the subject who was both articulate and telegenic. There had to be a "gee-whiz" visual (a sophisticated machine or eye-popping computer graphic, for example). There had to be some local angle to the story, in order to justify covering it on their local news broadcast. And, importantly, the reporter had to describe the breakthrough in layperson's terms that could be understood by any viewer with a tenth-grade education.

Finally, the document outlined the approximate cost of deploying a reporting team and provided guidelines about expense management, such as "If a story would require this much investment, it must be powerful enough to be the feature story that we advertise throughout the day."

In Step 2 of their process, the senior team compiled a list of "bad" stories the station had aired, and identified precisely what made them bad. From this exercise, several more criteria emerged, including:

The maximum length of any science or technology story must be under three minutes.

The story cannot include any visual that might make a viewer sick to his stomach, since our newscast is often watched near dinnertime.

No similar story can have aired on a competing local station within the past three months.

Finally, in Step 3, the senior team selected certain past story ideas, then paired them with the associated good and bad stories that were subsequently aired based upon them, and showed how elements of the original story ideas led to eventual success or failure of the final stories themselves. These signpost examples then served as models for the junior staffers to use in the future.

You can follow these same three steps. The presentation of your "template" doesn't have to be elaborate. But if the content is clear, you'll see an immediate improvement in the quality of the suggestions made by your junior staffers.

TEACHING THE BRAINSTEERING APPROACH

To teach others to be sources of ideas using Brainsteering, build on the foundation you established in leading your students through their first Brainsteering workshop, as described in Chapter 7. Based on that experience, they should already have faith that a question-based approach leads to good ideas, *for them.* Your job now is to lead them—at the right pace—through the process of learning three new skills: generating original questions to build their personal arsenals; becoming more rigorous through the use of logic trees; and moving skillfully back and forth between ideation and analysis. Their journey will be similar to the one you took in Chapters 3, 4, and 5.

A few observations, based on our own teaching experience, may help you with that process. First, if you haven't already done so in the course of holding Brainsteering workshops, avoid exposing your students to your full library of questions too early. Instead, ask them to begin generating questions from their own observations of the best (relevant) innovations and ideas they've seen in the past. You want them to stretch those intellectual muscles. Our experience has been that students who gain access to a large library of questions too early never become very good at creating original questions. We don't know whether that's due to intellectual laziness or being intimidated ("My teacher has accumulated a lot of knowledge and experience here. I can't possibly hope to match her in my early attempts, so I'll play it safe"). But we *do* know that you'll have more success if you force them to find new questions on their own before opening up your library to them—and yes, we say that despite the expectation that most of the questions they "invent" will already reside somewhere in your library.

Second, don't be afraid to subject your students' ideas to tough qualitative scrutiny right from the beginning, using the techniques we discussed in the first blush analysis portion of Chapter 5 and evaluating them against the baseline standard of success you'll have developed as a result of the prior section of this chapter. Remember how participants in a Brainsteering workshop are supposed to iterate and improve their ideas during each individual thirty-minute ideation session? That happens much more rapidly and effectively if your students have internalized the ability to analyze and judge ideas for themselves.

Third, when you introduce the concept of logic trees, again force your students to develop their own before exposing them to many "official" versions. Here, for the reasons we discussed in Chapter 4, you should expect significant originality in tree designs—and that's good. Once they master the technique, each student's logic trees will bring a different, and usually insightful, perspective to supplement any trees you've already been using. Just be sure to check that your students have learned to produce trees that are MECE and logically simple.

Finally, you'll be in a position to teach the students the various process components of the Brainsteering approach—again, in the same order as the flow of the book: individual skills first, then how to lead others through effective Brainsteering workshops.

DELEGATING APPROPRIATELY

As our magazine editor friends described at the outset of this chapter, turning over critical tasks to people you believe aren't ready yet seems like folly. Therefore, teaching involves finding the right balance of risk—too little and your people will never develop, too much and you'll have a disaster on your hands.

Fortunately, there are two keys to delegating appropriately in a creative environment. The first is to learn how to take "controlled quality risks." In a controlled situation, the actual risk you're running is not equal to the risk that your young subordinates might fail. If you have the time and personal capacity to recover from their failure without it becoming your failure, or if you can absorb their failure with little consequence, then your actual risk is limited. Therefore, you run a controlled quality risk if you: (1) assign your people only tasks that you're confident they can perform (hardly a model for growth); (2) keep the expected number of failures below the number you have the capacity to fix; or (3) assign tasks that can't actually damage you too much if they're not performed well.

The second key is to ensure that students will actually take the risks you're willing to bear—otherwise they'll never learn. The stereotypical picture we've all been taught to expect is that of a student feeling his oats and a teacher afraid of the student running amok, causing untold damage. In our experience, though, the opposite happens just as frequently: the teacher wants students to experiment with new ideas or to stretch the boundaries of the freedom given to them, but they respond too conservatively. They continue to take the safe path.

How do you find the right middle ground? By creating a shared understanding of the acceptable and unacceptable behaviors—and failures—that you expect of your people at each stage of the training. With a couple of hours of solid thinking, those expectations can be codified, even for people in creative jobs, where conventional wisdom has often held "You can't boil creative things down to a template or checklist!"

One advertising agency did just that for a position many people had previously considered "un-codifiable" and "un-gradable"—the copywriter. (In an advertising agency, the ideas for ads are typically developed by a team consisting of a copywriter who writes the words— "copy"—for the ad and an art director who designs the visuals.)

Previously, the skills of junior copywriters had been judged primarily on the gut feelings of the more senior copywriters. Coaching had been even more spotty; the prevailing mood among many of the seniors was "a copywriter either has it or she doesn't."

Despite some initial reluctance and doubts, the seniors discovered that with only a little bit of effort, they were actually able to articulate quite clearly their expectations of junior copywriters along several key dimensions of performance. On the opposite page is a (simplified) version of their output, describing their expectations with respect to three particularly important dimensions: concept origination, concept creativity, and use of language.

Using this grid, all junior members of the copywriting staff now know how much freedom they have to explore. They also know how expectations of them will increase over time, and what skill levels they'll have to demonstrate to be eligible for promotion. If an intern always responds to an assignment by sticking strictly to the current ad concept, he runs little risk of failure—but he'll also never grow past that point. On the other hand, if another intern never seeks guidance and regularly returns with ad concepts that depart entirely from those previously agreed to by the client, she can be coached about avoiding those choices where she doesn't yet have the experience to effectively judge the trade-off between value and risk.

Even creative jobs can be objectively evaluated

SKILL GRADING CRITERIA FOR JUNIOR COPYWRITERS

	Copywriting Intern	Early Tenure Copywriter	Mid Tenure Copywriter	Ready for Advancement
Concept Origination	Follows client's intent and sees implications for ad concepts	Consistently refines rough ad concepts into polished ones	Helps client better articulate value of product, and translates into new concepts for individual ads	Spots unrecognized value in product, and translates into new concepts for entire ad campaigns
Concept Creativity	Refines previously agreed-upon ad concepts	Offers original, sound variations on accepted ad concepts; effectively builds on others' ideas	Consistently and independently generates strong, original concepts of individual ads within existing campaign	Originates novel, practical concepts for entire ad campaigns
Use of Language	Conveys core messages clearly and concisely, with appropriate grammar	Writes copy that reflects and enhances the voice and point of view of each speaker	Adjusts rhythm and pace of copy to shape audience's mood appropriately	Creates memorable and "catchy" phrases that capture audience with wit, charm, emotion

Finally, encourage wise risk taking, but don't remove all consequences of failure. Really stupid failures shouldn't be tolerated, and marginally stupid ones should legitimately impede career progress. (After all, you're not running the place solely for the benefit of your trainees.)

OVERCOMING YOUR RELUCTANCE TO PROVIDING FEEDBACK

Okay, let's be honest. *We* know that *you* know that you can't teach others to be sources of creative ideas without giving them feedback. And *you* know that *we* know that you still don't do it very often or very well. So: how are we going to help you improve your situation?

Not by giving you a basic lesson on how to give effective coaching and feedback. There are plenty of great books on that subject. Instead, let's try to get to the heart of the issue: *why you aren't currently doing it*. Then you can apply your existing knowledge—and the lessons from all those other books—all day long.

Why don't managers of people in creative jobs like giving coaching and feedback? For starters, let's acknowledge that most managers of people in *any* kind of job don't like it either, so the problem is universal. But frankly, the problem truly is worse in the case of managers charged with leading people in creative jobs.

In our experience, such people—we'll call them "Creative Types"—receive less coaching and feedback than other kinds of workers due to one of three managerial excuses: one that's a travesty of management theory from the 1980s, one based upon unfounded embarrassment at implied egotism, and one tracing to an overblown fear of experiencing a meltdown. Let's eliminate each one in turn.

Excuse #1: "Less Is More"

Every once in a while, life lets you off the hook. Someone publishes a study that essentially says that something you didn't really want to do would have been bad for you anyway. Like "too much exercise ruins your joints."

In the 1970s and 1980s, the findings of some early psychological research on motivation and creativity were both oversimplified and taken out of context to create a false prescription for managing Creative Types: "Do nothing."[1] Supposedly, imposing any form of external motivation, constraints, evaluation, or feedback would hurt their creative output.

That prescription shot through the ranks of managers everywhere like proof that broccoli causes cancer would shoot through a second-grade classroom ("Hey, Mom! Look at *this*!"). We saw it in business school textbooks, suffered through speeches about it by a variety of so-called experts, and heard it repeated by several bosses and by client after client.

Please. Forget you ever heard that travesty. First, it was never an accurate depiction of the original research findings. Second, subsequent research by current Harvard professor Teresa Amabile and others has modified and improved our collective understanding of the impact of management levers on creativity.[2] And third, as a manager, your goal for your subordinates in most cases is not pure, unbridled creativity for its own sake, but *applied* creativity. Constraints are real. Product designs must be delivered on time and meet the specs of what customers will pay for. The cost of shooting the new ad campaign must fit within the client's available resources. And so on.

So don't assuage your guilt by relying on misinformed, outdated advice from the 1980s. You have no academically supported excuse for avoiding giving coaching and feedback to your Creative Types.

Excuse #2: "Says Who?"

Most managers believe creative work is hard to define and measure, so they often feel less legitimate than they should about telling a Creative Type, "Your work isn't as good as you think it is, or as good as it needs to be." They fear the potential retort, *"Says who?"* because they feel embarrassed at the apparent egotism of their implied response: "I do, and my opinion is more legitimate than yours."

Turn your thinking around.

First, take advantage of the tool you developed based on the previous section of this chapter—the skill grading criteria grid—to remove the feeling that this discussion consists of two people who are simply sharing vague and equally valid opinions. A good grid provides an objective, experienced-based set of standards that enable you to establish expectations with your charges and then accurately compare the quality of their work against those standards.

We've been inside organizations when they implemented such grids, and we've seen firsthand that this tool can completely change the content, tone, and value of coaching and feedback discussions. For the first time, there's an agreed-upon standard. That standard is now outside of the person giving the feedback, even if that person was its inventor. The conversation becomes one of "which statement best describes the quality of this person's work on each criterion?"

So create the grid. Tell your subordinates ahead of time that these are the standards against which their work will be judged. Figure out before the feedback session which statements on the grid best describe their performance and—very important—why you believe their current work does not yet qualify for the next-higher-level statement, complete with a few examples.

Second, remember that your opinion about how well your subordinate has performed against the grid is objectively superior to his. Yes, compared to many other kinds of work, creative work *is* harder to define and measure in absolute terms. But your role as a boss/teacher is not to judge your subordinate/student's intrinsic creativity, but to judge how well he applied his creative skills to a particular task.

You know more about that task than he does. You've dealt with such tasks for longer than he has. You succeeded at those tasks so well that you got promoted. So remember that your review is not about "pure art" (about which some recent trends in art appreciation claim that any one person's opinion is no more valid than anyone else's), but about applied creativity. Compared to your student, your opinion actually *is* better—it better predicts which product will succeed in the marketplace, which TV script will attract better ratings, which phrasing will most excite potential buyers, and so on.

Excuse #3: "Just Shoot Me"

The population of Creative Types seems to contain more than its fair share of emotionally sensitive souls, and such people can be especially difficult to deliver feedback to. You can debate whether these folks were simply born insecure, or have been made insecure by being unfairly judged against fuzzy standards for so many years. You can also debate whether their emotional sensitivity is actually a good thing or a bad thing depending on the nature of their particular job. What you can't debate is this: deep down, you know you often avoid giving feedback to Creative Types because you fear that somewhere, sometime, you'll have to deal with The Meltdown or its cousin, The Blowup.

The Meltdown "Oh my God! You're right! My work is *trash*. I don't deserve to be here—in fact, I never did. My life is ruined—but it was worthless anyway. I'll quit now and save you the trouble of firing me. Maybe I can get a job painting lawn statues—that's all I'm really good for."

The Blowup "What do you *mean* my work isn't great? You wouldn't know great if it came with a blue ribbon attached to it! I'm going somewhere where my genius is appreciated. I quit!"

Both reactions can be quite amusing when viewed from a safe distance, but not while they're happening to *you*. (Of course, the same can be said for a lot of things. When our older brother was a toddler, our mother took him to the grocery store. Sitting in the shopping cart as they cruised down an aisle, he playfully picked up a carton of eggs and flung it to the floor—breaking all the eggs, of course. A very proper gentleman standing just beyond the splash zone burst out laughing. Indignant, Mom glared at him and said sternly, "I fail to see what's so amusing." Came the reply: "That, madam, is because it's *your* child.")

We know of many cases where the subconscious fear of being on the receiving end of a Meltdown or a Blowup has caused managers to avoid giving performance appraisals to *anyone* for years.

But the truth is, you can't let the possibility of such reactions (or even their milder variants) prevent you from being an effective manager. Start by identifying which few of your workers might possibly go off the deep end—then give feedback to everyone else. Worst case, even if you chicken out on the few, you won't fail to offer coaching to the many. Best case, you'll build your confidence by practicing on the normal many, and then have the courage to deal with the remaining, more volatile few. Steel your nerves and go for it.

9

Creating an Idea Factory

The better you become at producing ideas of your own and at leading others to develop ideas, the more ideas you'll be asked to produce. And at some point, you'll be asked to run "the idea factory." Maybe you'll get promoted to department head, or maybe your job scope will be expanded to include a creative team or two. Or maybe you'll just be given a whole new assignment ("Ed's good at that 'new idea' thing—maybe *he* can manage that unruly mob of wackos"). Whatever the reason, at some point you'll want to help your organization crank out more and better ideas, time after time.

In an idea factory, idea generation isn't a one-time episode, it's an ongoing challenge requiring a steady production line of new and better ideas. It's a fact of life for an R&D lab that supports a large number of product lines. It holds true for a Web designer whose every Web site must look and feel unique. It's all-day-every-day for a catalog retailer who must find new and interesting ways to photograph four products per page in a hundred-page catalog four times a year. And it's that job we discussed in Chapter 5, writing TV scripts for a one-hour drama.

In idea factories, one great idea—or even twenty great ideas—won't make you successful. Not by a long shot. You need good idea after good idea after good idea. And to exacerbate your problem, you're probably on deadline. The catalog is going in the mail on April 17, whether the photos are good or bad. The TV show will air next Thursday at 9:00 p.m., whether you're ready or not.

So what should you do?

One thing you probably should *not* do is waste your time asking for additional resources; odds are, you won't get them. Our experience across many for-profit industries and in a variety of not-for-profit settings indicates that few institutions value new ideas highly enough to support requests for additional spending just to find more of them. In fact, the long-term trend across many sectors of the economy in recent years (even before the Great Recession) has been to *shrink* staff sizes, including the number of creative positions.

Nope, the thing to do is add some more tools to your Brainsteering toolkit. We hope the tools and techniques you've already taken away from this book—the arsenal of Right Questions you've developed, the comprehensive logic trees you now know how to build, the dramatically improved process for drawing new ideas from your coworkers in a Brainsteering workshop, and so on—have already helped you substantially increase both the volume and the quality of new ideas you're producing. But to help you create a virtually endless stream of ideas, you need a few more. Specifically, you must learn how to:

Formalize the ideation process.

Expand your sources of Right Questions.

Institutionalize your inventory of Right Questions.

Avoid falling into unhealthy patterns.

Periodically rejuvenate the entire system.

FORMALIZING THE IDEATION PROCESS

In a production-line-of-ideas setting, you won't be present when most ideation sessions are held, when most ideas are selected for implementation, or when most people are coached. Therefore, you must systematize the tools and techniques you've learned, so that they'll be just as effective in other people's hands as they are in yours. In that light, let's revisit three key topics:

Ensuring that everyone understands what's expected
Employing a more formal decision-making process
"Officially" adopting the Brainsteering process

Ensure that everyone understands what's expected

Your first step is to formally codify and communicate the baseline standards and criteria for performance that you developed in Chapter 8. That means writing them down, sending out copies to your entire creative team, and taking the time to discuss them with everyone whom you expect to generate ideas. Once you initially publish the standards, be sure to keep them fresh and up-to-date, and take steps to ensure that every new member of your team is thoroughly "indoctrinated" early in their tenure.

Our consulting alma mater, McKinsey & Company, provides an excellent example of creating and communicating clear performance standards to idea workers. In his or her first two weeks with the firm, every single consultant is taught that his or her performance on every client project will be evaluated on a standardized grid that is analogous to (but much more comprehensive than) the one we showed you in Chapter 8. And that's exactly what happens, several times each year. The results from these individual client project reviews are then aggregated into semiannual reviews in which the consultant's progress is compared to standardized expectations at that consultant's stage in the career path. The semiannual reviews drive compensation and promotion decisions, and provide excellent opportunities for rigorous, valuable coaching. In short, everyone knows the drill, and everyone adheres to it.

Employ a more formal decision-making process

If your factory is large enough, you may be faced with multiple decision-making bodies, each with its own (unofficial and potentially renegade) set of criteria and dynamics. Further, some frontline idea generators may finish their work sooner than others. Your decision makers may then find it difficult to act on one set of options when they don't know what other options will surface later. Or one set of recommendations made today may be contingent on a presumed choice that will not be made until later.

To mitigate these issues, you may need to employ a more formal decision-making process—which means centrally specifying a single set of rules everyone must follow. Formulating rules is easy; the secret to success, though, lies in striking the right balance between the rigidity of your rules and the need to allow lower levels of decision makers the freedom to adjust those rules to their unique circumstances.

As always, there is no single magic answer. But in general, the right balance depends on the weight you place on each subunit judging ideas in exactly the same way. If the goal of every subunit is identical, then you'll want strict adherence to your criteria. Achieving the same level of adherence as the size of your factory increases will require more formality in the decision process. Moreover, the less pleasant the choices are, the more formality you'll need in the decision process to ensure adherence.

But be warned. In a sign that the gods of management have a sense of irony, those who will be governed by your process will use these very same factors to argue that your process should be made *more* flexible, not less. The larger your organization, the more likely it is that different subunits of the organization will face radically different situations—and consequently, the more likely it is that any one process might be inappropriate for some subunit. And the more unpleasant the task, the greater the potential for adverse reactions among your employees to a process that may seem arbitrary and inflexible when viewed from their standpoint.

On one level, those employees are right. But our experience tells us, overwhelmingly, that more flexibility in any decision-making process inevitably results in lower adherence to any one particular set of goals (in this case, *your* goals). It's a trade-off that only you can make. Just be careful.

"Officially" adopt the Brainsteering process

The common practice in idea factories is to think of ideation as an individual art, and therefore allow each person or subunit within the organization to find their own preferred approach to generating ideas. The result is a patchwork of approaches among different subteams.

When running an idea factory, especially one that involves more than a handful of people, we strongly encourage you to "officially" designate a single approach for all of your teams, whether or not that approach is Brainsteering. You can still allow other approaches as supplements, but you should want all your subunits to migrate toward a single core approach as their base style.

Why? Because a single approach allows the maximum leverage of discoveries and improvements. It facilitates training, promotes learning, and enables easier movement of people among subunits. Further, if everyone uses a similar approach, then a discovery in one team (such as of a killer Right Question, or a better evaluation standard) can immediately benefit every subunit. That's not the case if you have a patchwork of approaches. Any discovery that improves one approach will likely be irrelevant to those using a significantly different approach. (In fact, under a patchwork system, the discovery is unlikely to benefit even those to whom it could be relevant, because any given subunit won't fully understand the approaches being used by other teams and therefore may not even know whether or not to pass along their discovery.)

As to which approach to adopt, you might reasonably assume that we're biased toward Brainsteering over any other. But the truth is that our review of the currently available innovation literature failed to find any other equally integrated approach for consistently generating new ideas. Thus, if you believe our argument that there are important gains to be made from an integrated approach . . .

EXPANDING YOUR SOURCES OF RIGHT QUESTIONS

Because an idea factory must produce so many ideas, it constantly needs new sources for those ideas. Therefore, in this situation, you can't afford to ignore any high-payoff source of new questions. But oddly, we constantly find idea factories where people have overlooked some obvious sources of ideas.

First ask yourself whether you've properly mined your own institutional history. Typically, idea-centric institutions do the opposite. For reasons we won't discuss here, idea factory organizations tend to have high rates of turnover. This in turn causes them to inadvertently purge their own institutional memory. How often have you been in a meeting where you hear someone say, "You know, we used to . . . but then we kind of got away from doing that"?

Therein lies a major opportunity. If, as is typical, your organization has never mined its own files for sources of ideas, do it now. If your organization is in the media, have interns read old issues or watch your old episodes, or listen to the songs you never sold. If you run an advertising agency, schedule a day for everyone to review historical reels of your greatest campaigns. If you work for a consulting firm, reread the old classic proposals in your field. You may want to copy some of the specific ideas contained in your organization's past work products. More important, you will definitely gain from reverse engineering the questions that led to those ideas, as we taught you to do back in Chapter 2. Every successful institution has a history of ideas that have been lost. It's only your creative pride that prevents you from mining that history.

Once you've done that, have the creative humility to steal the best ideas of others.

Start by investigating the successful innovations of organizations that conduct your business in other geographies, or that are similar to but different from your organization in some key respect, such as serving similar customers, using similar processes or technologies, and so on. Steal their ideas.

Oh, don't feel bad—you won't be the first to "borrow" a huge idea. Not by a long shot. Take *Guitar Hero*, the hit video game in which the player plays a much simplified guitar while watching a much simplified set of musical notes scroll past on his TV screen in sync with a recording of a famous rock song. The *Guitar Hero* series of games has sold more than 25 million copies since its introduction in 2005—that's over $2 billion in sales. Its publisher claims that the series' third release (*Guitar Hero III: Legends of Rock*) is the first single video game to exceed $1 billion in sales.[1]

So where did *Guitar Hero*'s inventors get such a great idea? They lifted it from Japan. The game is a very close copy of *GuitarFreaks*, an arcade game invented by the Konami Corporation that was popular in Japan in the early and mid-2000s. The idea for a simplified guitar? Lifted from Konami. Visual guidance? Konami. Playing along with famous songs? Konami. Lead *Guitar Hero* designer Rob Kay has even been quoted as saying, "[The company] was interested in making a guitar game, as they'd seen *GuitarFreaks*, which Konami had done."[2]

Lest you think that stealing creative ideas is beneath you, or that you're so leading-edge that the rest of the world simply follows you, consider Hollywood.

Hollywood is widely acknowledged as the center of the television universe, and it's justly proud that it originates the largest single share of new ideas of any creative community in the whole TV business. But get this: both of the top-rated U.S. television shows of 2009, *American Idol* and *Dancing with the Stars*, are actually copies of British television shows—*Pop Idol* and *Strictly Come Dancing*, respectively.[3] As was *Who Wants to Be a Millionaire?*, the top-rated show of the 1999–2000 season.[4] Even in earlier times, *All in the Family*, the number one show from 1971 to 1976, was a copy of the British series *'Til Death Us Do Part*.[5] In the interests of fairness, we need to point out that these cases weren't complete "steals"—in most cases, the original British producers were involved in the American versions (some more directly than others). But the point is the same.

Once you've gotten comfortable with the idea of stealing ideas *in general*, take the next dose of humility and ask yourself what you can steal from your direct competitors. Yes, we know that yours is the leading company in its field; that your competitors look to you for innovations, not vice versa; and that their products are pale imitations of your own and are inferior in every way possible. Get over it. Steal ideas from them anyway—but be smarter in how you do it. Stealing their product features is pedestrian; you really want to steal their intellectual models—as in, what are the Right Questions *they* ask?

To illustrate, let's go back to Hollywood and move across the celluloid street from TV shows to feature films. A few years ago, someone hit on a bullet proof formula for producing a profitable film:

Step 1: Ask, "What subgroup of teenagers is extremely enthusiastic about participating in an activity that the rest of their peers do *not* think is cool—and who, therefore, have not been portrayed favorably in the movies to date? Or better yet, have not been portrayed at all?"

Step 2: Write a script that celebrates how dedicated these participants must be to succeed at their chosen avocation, how much strength of character is required, and how those kids are actually cool in their own way.

Step 3: Hire great-looking (but relatively unknown and therefore inexpensive) actors and actresses to play those role models in a movie.

The producers' business plan calls for the movie to attract a narrow base of truly fanatical kids who will come to see it multiple times—and preferably drag along their friends and family members. As long as the producers know the size of the participant base or fan base for the featured activity at the center of the movie, they can reasonably predict the order-of-magnitude revenues achievable. Then they just have to control costs accordingly. Fortunately, these movies can be relatively inexpensive to make, because unknown actors plus no exotic locations plus stock footage of the crowd scenes plus no special effects equals cheap.

Okay, let's now look at a brief history of successful "thefts" of this formula. The first (albeit incomplete) application of the formula may well have been *Revenge of the Nerds*, released in 1984 by Twentieth Century Fox, followed by *Revenge of the Nerds II: Nerds in Paradise* in 1987. In those early days, it seems the formula was still under development. The target audience might not have been "extremely enthusiastic" about conducting the activities of a nerd, and the nerds in the movie weren't exactly beautiful—they looked more like übernerds. But the rest of the formula worked. The production budget for the first movie was $8 million, and it achieved box office revenues of $41 million. The sequel tacked on another $30 million in revenues—and neither of those figures counts subsequent VCR or DVD sales.[6] A tidy profit, no?

Next up: 1992's *The Cutting Edge*, released by MGM. (Note that this one had different producers and was released by a different studio. As we said, don't hesitate to steal from your competitors.) The target audience: amateur figure skaters—especially aspiring young female figure skaters—and their fans. We haven't found its production budget, but a quick viewing of the movie will assure you that it must have been pretty small. Nonetheless, the film generated U.S. box office receipts of $25 million (again, not counting VCR/DVD sales), and went on to spawn not just one but two sequels.[7]

The formula was getting closer to perfection—but wait, there's more. The pinnacle had yet to be reached. Flash forward to the year 2000. Yet another team of producers, working with yet another studio, Universal, creates *Bring It On*, a movie about competitive cheerleading. The formula is now complete. Competitive cheerleaders absolutely meet the "extremely enthusiastic" standard, and the then little-known actresses and actors are beautiful and inexpensive. *Bring It On* achieves total box office revenues of over $90 million (with VCR/DVD sales far beyond that) against a production cost of $28 million.[8] The film becomes a cult classic—outside of the United States, American-style cheerleading is now often referred to as *Bring It On*–style cheerleading. The movie not only (pun alert!) catapults Kirsten Dunst to a whole new level of career success in Hollywood; it also generates *four* sequels (or, as some critics called them, copies): 2004's *Bring It On Again*; 2006's *Bring It On: All or Nothing*; 2007's *Bring It On: In It to Win It*; and 2009's *Bring It On: Fight to the Finish*.

"So now that the formula has been perfected with cheerleading," asked a few enterprising individuals racking their brains one day in L.A., "what *other* groups of maligned teens can we identify?" Marching bands, for starters. In 2002, yet another different group of producers gave the world *Drumline*, released by Twentieth Century Fox (*finally*, a studio savvy enough to steal one of its own past ideas; remember who originally pioneered this formula by bringing you *Revenge of the Nerds*?). Produced for $20 million, the film achieved box office of $58 million (again, not including DVD sales).[9]

How about young female gymnasts? They're certainly enthusiastic. The 2006 film was called *Stick It*, released by (say it with us, now) yet another studio, Touchstone Pictures. Grossed $32 million at the box office.[10] And the television show that follows "the formula" and is aimed at the same crowd? It's called *Make It or Break It*, produced by ABC Family, which happens to be owned by The Walt Disney Company, parent of—you guessed it—Touchstone Pictures.

Wait, did we say television could also steal the formula? That might explain *Glee*, the multi-award-winning series that first sang and danced its way across TV screens in 2009, produced by Twentieth Century Fox Television (notice the connection?). It celebrates yet another group of overlooked, often disrespected—but extremely enthusiastic—teens: those who sing in high school choirs and glee clubs.

Okay, so this particular formula doesn't lead to *Avatar*, but it's still a pretty good business model. (By the way: *Avatar*, too, is actually another example of a stolen formula—just not this one.)

If Hollywood can steal the best ideas of others, so can you. Again, it's only your creative pride that holds you back.

INSTITUTIONALIZING YOUR INVENTORY OF RIGHT QUESTIONS

Given the volume of ideas that you need to generate every month, each team in your factory needs a long list of Right Questions to choose from, more than they can likely develop on their own even with the benefit of (ahem) "expanded sources" as shown above. Therefore, teams must be able to share ideas—and that means having a central database. Of course, institutionalizing such an inventory means more than just establishing a onetime compilation of questions. Any central database must be carefully organized if it's going to be useful; if your teams can't find the relevant Right Questions within your database, then you're effectively in the same place as if you had no database.

To build and maintain a truly great database, each subunit within your organization must feel an obligation to regularly deposit new knowledge, not just be a free rider on the system. That will not happen automatically. You'll have to work the problem by, for example, making it a component of your performance expectations. You'll also need to appoint someone (or if you have a large enough organization, a couple of someones) to catalog new entries, throw out duplicates, and remove any questions that once seemed helpful but have proved to be duds. Otherwise your database will become cluttered and useless, then gradually fall apart as people stop using it.

All of the leading consulting firms have such systems. Every consultant has open access to a common database of proprietary knowledge regarding project approaches, points of view about industries and functions, and so on. These pearls of wisdom are analogous to the Right Questions and logic trees that lie at the heart of this book. As consultants advance in their careers, every one of them is expected to both tap into that database regularly and contribute to it. In fact, one's contributions to the database are factored into promotion decisions. Full-time administrators manage the database, culling out entries that are redundant, have been superseded, or have been judged less useful for any other reason. The database imposes a significant cost on the firms, but it confers a powerful competitive advantage.

AVOIDING UNHEALTHY PATTERNS

A typical problem of any production-line-of-ideas organization is the tendency to fall into patterns. Let's say one particular approach—like using a certain Right Question—produces a great result once or twice. Then whenever the idea workers are stumped for an idea, or a deadline is approaching, they consciously or unconsciously return to that same safe solution. Later, newer staffers witness the frequency with which the organization uses that approach, and assume that it forms part of the "style" of the place. Before long, your factory becomes repetitive.

Of course, every individual and organization develops certain patterns over time, because we all have biases. The issue is whether those patterns are healthy or unhealthy.

Patterns can be unhealthy for a number of reasons. First, going down the same thought path will degrade the quality of the ideas themselves and/or cause you to invest progressively more and more effort to develop ideas of similar power. (Remember the Innovation S-curve from Chapter 2?) Second, if your idea factory produces ideas that fill only a subset of the available possibilities, you have by definition left gaps for competitors to fill. Why give them a free shot? Third, if output has become repetitious, it's potentially predictable and boring—a dangerous thing for any idea factory. Finally, and most important, if your organization is dedicated to creativity, why would you settle for being anything less than you could be?

Ask yourself: Do a disproportionate number of your product ideas focus on the biggest hassle? Do they keep trying to meet the unmet needs of the same subset of users? Do your cost reduction ideas too often center on identifying people who process paper and replacing them with electronic methods, when the larger opportunities might lie in simply addressing underperformers?

Fortunately, in Chapter 4 we introduced you to a great tool for avoiding these problems: logic trees. There we used trees to find holes in your thinking. Now we'll use them to diagnose repetitive patterns in your thinking. This will give you a tool for seeing whether you've pushed past the point of diminishing returns on a single tool or technique or issue.

To find patterns, simply create a sound logic tree, just as you did in Chapter 4, then count the number of ideas your organization has used that resulted from each branch of the tree in whatever time period you believe is relevant. We've used periods as short as two months in the case of a media client, and as long as three years in the case of product enhancements in consumer durables industries.

As a specific, quantifiable, but easily digested example, let's return to a familiar real-world idea factory challenge we visited in Chapter 4: media coverage of celebrities. We recently analyzed the pattern of ninety-two feature stories published in *People* magazine over a nine-week period in late 2009.[11] The results are tabulated below.

Logic trees can help identify healthy and unhealthy patterns in your thinking

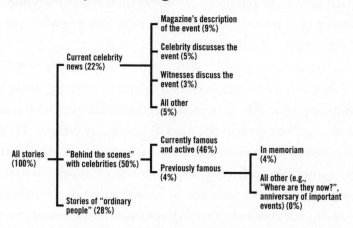

Figure 9.1: Analysis Of 92 Feature Stories Appearing In *People* Magazine, August–December 2009

Some interesting patterns emerge. First, you'll note that *People* magazine is not really a celebrity gossip magazine to anything like the degree you might expect. Fewer than a quarter of its stories

(22 percent) actually rely on current celebrity news. Fully half of its stories (50 percent) take advantage of the magazine's relationships with celebrities to go behind the scenes into their personal lives. And over a quarter of its stories (28 percent) actually don't concern celebrities at all, but ordinary people about whom an interesting story can be told.

Next, *People* appears to stick with an "at the moment" perspective to a significant degree. It rarely discusses stars whose fame has faded (4 percent)—and even then, only if the former celebrity is currently in the news for having died.

Finally, when *People* does cover current celebrity news, the magazine seems to prefer to stay very close to the event itself, as opposed to writing backstories or how this event compares to those involving other celebrities.

People's editors might be very happy with these patterns. After all, some patterns are healthy. (You'll remember from Chapter 3 that for any given task, some questions *are* better than others.) But notice that the pattern does provide some insights as to how *People*'s competitors could differentiate themselves.

First, competitors could boast that they are "all-celebrity" magazines if they believe certain readers aren't very interested in the stories of ordinary people. Or they could regularly feature "whatever happened to . . . ?" reunions of the casts of old, wildly popular TV shows. Or they could adopt a more speculative approach to covering celebrity events, opening up such story angles as "what will happen next?" and "things the star doesn't want you to know." Such policies help explain why newsstands routinely carry simultaneous editions of magazines featuring directly contradictory cover stories about the state of Brad Pitt and Angelina Jolie's relationship.

So analyze your own factory's idea patterns, and then analyze the patterns of your competitors. You'll almost always notice something interesting. Is the quality of ideas that originate in one branch declining over time? If so, avoid that branch for a while. Which branches do you rarely or never use? These can be opportunities for new perspectives and ideas. Which branches do you consciously or unconsciously avoid, even as your competitors exploit them? If you find any, make a conscious decision whether to continue ceding that space to your competitors or to challenge them more directly. And so on.

PERIODICALLY REJUVENATING THE ENTIRE SYSTEM

Every once in a while, even in the best idea factories, it's time to rejuvenate the entire system, to reach under the organization's metaphorical bed and clear out the dust bunnies.

At some point in the life of any idea factory, your team's output will seem just a little stale. You'll insist that you've employed and deployed the techniques in this book faithfully. And you'll have resorted to your Management 101 tricks more often than you'd like to admit. When you feel such an organizational hardening of the arteries coming on, it's time to act in either or both of two ways: by reorganizing and/or by deliberately "changing the formula."

Reorganize

That's right. Arbitrarily reorganize your idea-generation team. You'll recall that, back in Chapter 2, we introduced you to the notion that asking the identical question in the identical situation—but asking it of a different person—will elicit different ideas. When your team's output gets stale, it's time to do just that, on a larger scale.

We won't pretend to tell you exactly how to reorganize. You know your situation and your players better than we do. And frankly, for idea-generation purposes, the precise scheme you use may not matter. You just need to do *something* different. Who has been playing what roles on your ideation team? Change them.

Deliberately change the formula

Despite all the ideas in this chapter to help you generate a wide variety of ideas (including reorganizing), the eventual fate of any idea factory is virtually certain: sooner or later, you'll exhaust the full potential of the core concept of your business. The Innovation S-curve *will* eventually catch up with you. At that point, it will be time to deliberately change the formula—to throw out the standards, throw out the catalog of questions you've been using, and rethink everything.

It's been done many times (and not just by pop singer Madonna, who may hold the world record for extending a career in entertainment by constantly reinventing herself). Gossip magazines had to rethink their concept as television entertainment programs and the Internet stole their ability to be the first communicator of celebrity news. TV news has been reinvented several times. The consulting and legal industries are both involved in major reinvention today.

And even though we criticized FedEx for its ZapMail initiative, it is to be credited for at least seeing that electronic transmission technologies would undercut its market for overnight delivery of small documents, which constituted a large portion of its total business at the time, and trying to do something about that before it became extinct. FedEx subsequently did a remarkable job of reorienting its business toward just-in-time delivery of small parts and other packages that by definition required physical delivery, and maintained an enviable growth record over the years. For example, FedEx Express (the portion of the company that handles the delivery of small parts and such) grew 84 percent in the ten years between 1998 and 2008.[12]

Again, we're not going to take up your time by telling you exactly how to change your particular formula; if you've gotten this far in the book, you already know how. But we *will* give you this warning: the reaction of many people around you will be that you shouldn't abandon the successful formula you're already following, and that "you're wasting your time by trying to reinvent the wheel."

Don't listen to them. Reinventing the wheel has gotten a bum rap. If you stop and think about it, the wheel has actually been reinvented many times over the ages—and each time to great effect. It's likely that the first "wheels" were actually logs placed on the ground, over which very heavy objects were pushed and made to roll forward. The wheel was reinvented to be massively lighter when it was made less wide than high, and again when two wheels were connected by an axle. It was made even better when mankind learned how to make it from multiple wooden parts rather than a single block of wood or stone. Later, it became still lighter when it was "hollowed out," replacing a solid mass with a combination of rim and spokes. Then someone thought to surface the wheel's rim with a shock-absorbing material, followed by the hollow tire. Somewhere along the way, the rim of the wheel was modified to create an entirely new invention—the gear. And so on.

So don't listen to naysayers who may criticize you for trying to reinvent the wheel. Thank goodness others have done exactly that.

PART IV

THE GRAND FINALE

PART IV

10

Developing Your Own Billion-Dollar Idea

No serious book on inventing new ideas would be complete without at least a few thoughts on how to achieve the pinnacle of break-through ideas. And while there might be other worthy pinnacles out there (can you say Academy Award for Best Original Screenplay?), we have one particular candidate that our experience tells us is likely to be of great interest to many, many readers: the Billion-Dollar Idea.

Of course, we don't claim to know everything you need to know on this subject; if we did, we'd already have one of those private jets we keep referring to. That said, the Z–1–4 work we did at McKinsey examined, quite extensively, the patterns and key success requirements associated with launching just such an undertaking. So we hope we can provide you with some useful guidance. Heck, we might even throw in a couple of less than fully baked Billion-Dollar Idea examples along the way.

Simply stated, if you want to develop a Billion-Dollar Idea, you need to follow four principles:

Make a serious commitment—much more serious than you probably expect.

Take aim at a very large market.

Ramp up the intensity of the questions that you ask.

Be absolutely ruthless in your evaluation of the many ideas
you'll generate, before committing to the one you'll actually
implement.

Let's understand each of these in turn.

MAKE A SERIOUS COMMITMENT

The search for a Billion-Dollar Idea is a serious undertaking. The people who founded the Compaqs and Home Depots of the world were willing to bet the company (and often their own personal fortune) on their idea. In fact, by the time an average Z–1–4 company had broken even (at about fifteen months after start-up), its backers had invested an average of close to $119 million (in year 2000 dollars).

By contrast, most individuals—and organizations—approach idea generation casually, and, not surprisingly, achieve little in return. So before you even begin, ask yourself a few questions. And be unflinchingly honest in your answers.

Do you truly understand the likely scale and nature of the resources that would be required, and do you truly have access to them?

If you are even passingly familiar with the industry in which you hope to find and implement your Billion-Dollar Idea, you can probably make an order-of-magnitude guess at the investment that will eventually be required—even before you begin your search for the idea itself. For example, any billion-dollar product or service will inevitably require the expenditure of at least $100 million before reaching that revenue plateau. While it's true that early success can attract capital along the way, if you're part of a company that is either unable or unwilling to make large investments in your area, you should change goals.

A serious commitment is more than a strong desire. The difference hinges on the ability and willingness of those who control the necessary resources to take the necessary level of action. If you have the desire, but lack the necessary resources, you can't make a serious commitment.

Are you prepared for the time, cost, and frustration involved in the search?

Billion-Dollar Ideas are hard to find, and the search can be both time-consuming and frustrating. But don't be put off by that. Every Billion-Dollar Idea involves frustration.

Take what is arguably the most successful pop song ever written: "Yesterday," by Sir Paul McCartney of the Beatles. According to the Guinness World Records, "Yesterday" has the most cover versions of any song ever written. That is, more different artists have covered the song (by recording their own version of it) than any other song in history—over 3,000 versions in total.[1]

Broadcast Music Incorporated (BMI, one of the music industry organizations that monitor these things to make sure the creators of songs get paid what they are due) claims that "Yesterday" was performed over 7 million times between 1965 and 2000.[2] And the great thing for Sir Paul is that the entire melody came to him in a single dream. Sweet, right?

Ah, but the lyrics didn't come so easily. In fact, the song was originally nicknamed "Scrambled Eggs." (Could you imagine 3,000 cover versions of "Scrambled Eggs"? With Sir Paul's original working lyrics, which one source alleges were "Scrambled eggs/Have an omelet with some muenster cheese/Put your dishes in the wash bin, please/So I can clean the scrambled eggs"? Yeah, sure you can.)

Sir Paul once claimed that he had first written down "Yesterday" during the Beatles' tour of France in 1964. A year later, in 1965, he was still working on it—much to the annoyance of everyone around him.[3] During the shooting of the Beatles' famous movie *Help!*, McCartney constantly used a piano at the soundstage to work on the song. Richard Lester, the movie's director, eventually lost his temper, telling McCartney to stop or he would have the piano removed.[4] George Harrison complained: "Blimey, he's always talking about that song. You'd think he was Beethoven or somebody!" John Lennon concurred: "The song was around for months and months before we finally completed it. Every time we got together to write songs for a recording session, this one would come up."[5]

And when McCartney finally finished the song, did the other three Beatles jump to record it? Ummm, no. They thought it didn't suit their image. So it was first offered to a much lesser-known artist named Chris Farlowe—who promptly turned it down.[6]

Frustration is the unavoidable companion of many great ideas. William Golding's first novel, *Lord of the Flies*, was published in 1954. It eventually became a best seller, helped Golding win the Nobel Prize in Literature, and went on to be named in 2005 as one of *Time* magazine's "100 Best English Language Novels of All Time."[7] (Of note, the fine print in *Time*'s designation reveals that the magazine's definition of "all time" actually meant "since 1923," when *Time* magazine was first published—just in case you were wondering why *A Tale of Two Cities* and *Pride and Prejudice* failed to make the list.)

But don't assume that the creation of Golding's masterpiece was either quick or easy—*Lord of the Flies* was initially rejected by twenty-one publishers, and revised constantly along the way.[8] What's more, the twenty-second publisher agreed to go with it . . . only if Golding would revise it again. Ironically, later in his life, Golding announced that he hated the novel, although it's not clear whether he did so despite, or because of, all those revisions.[9]

You get the point. Be realistic. Do you have the hours available in your schedule, given your other responsibilities and commitments? Do you have the lead time necessary to obtain information, learn new subjects, schedule meetings far enough in advance? Will you be able to marshal the necessary financial resources—whether they come out of your own pocket or your organization's budget—to continue pushing ahead despite whatever setbacks occur? Are you willing to put up with long periods of frustration, and if you are working within the context of a larger organization, does it have the same degree of patience that you do?

Do you have a "sanity check" in place that can prevent you from fixating on a bad idea?

It's ironic: the more committed people or organizations are to achieving a big breakthrough, the more susceptible they are to Pygmalion's curse of falling in love with their own creation and failing to see its obvious flaws. Remember ZapMail and Webvan?

Recognize that, no matter how levelheaded you are, you're susceptible to the same biases as the unfortunate souls mentioned above—especially if you work for a large organization and are nearing the end of the time and budget limitations you've been given to conduct your search for a killer idea.

And don't count on the usual safety valves to protect you. In particular, don't count on members of your staff to point out the fact that the emperor is wearing no clothes. Why not? Because each of them privately knows that his or her career will be damaged less by being one of a hundred people vaguely associated with your failure than by being the one person who really, really upset you by pointing out the absurdity of your pet idea. (Remember the boss's idea about birthday cards from dead parents that we told you about in the introduction?)

In fact, sometimes it seems that the bigger your blunder, the less likely it is that your subordinates will step in and save you. We once sat in a room where forty senior people in the dominant division of one of the world's ten largest technology companies silently nodded their final approval of their leader's choice for a new product intended to revolutionize the division: "televisions for women" that would be painted pink and feature a simplified remote control. No one pointed out how patronizing the idea was. No one pointed out that, even though some women might not be as gadget-oriented as some men, they still place a higher premium on a TV's picture quality than on the color of its case, and this company had no advantage on picture quality. No one pointed out that there were already dramatically simplified remote controls on the market. And no one pointed out that, if by some chance pink TVs actually proved to be successful, the lead time required for competitors to copy their idea and introduce pink TVs of their own was very short indeed. Fortunately for the company (but not the executive in question), the CEO and board of directors were *not* reluctant to point out those things, and the idea soon died.

So for your own sake, if you want to search for a killer idea, be sure you keep someone around who's willing to say to you, "Colin, maybe you're right. Maybe it is actually a loon. But if it walks like a duck, and quacks like a duck . . . *for our purposes, it's a duck.*"

TAKE AIM AT A VERY LARGE MARKET

To state the obvious (for the first time in this entire book, of course), Billion-Dollar Ideas don't fit in small market niches. We're not turning up our noses at small market niches; you can make plenty of money by revolutionizing a small market, and it's easier to conquer a narrow niche than a broad one. But if you're reading this chapter, you're concerned only with Billion-Dollar Ideas, and they require a lot of room.

So if you're looking for a Billion-Dollar Idea, by all means find a niche—but look for a particularly valuable niche by revolutionizing some portion of a multibillion-dollar market.

We once conducted a Brainsteering workshop for a major American automobile company—let's call it "CarCo"—that was looking to boost its revenues by more than a billion dollars, through either new car sales or new businesses that were somehow related to its car business. One of the Right Questions we employed was "Who would otherwise buy our car, but doesn't buy it for one particular reason?" By the end of the first day, the client team had identified an interesting segment: a substantial group of young men who would be interested in buying CarCo's flagship sports car, except for the fact that their average monthly insurance premium for this car would be larger than the car payment itself.

Using this insight, we conducted a second Brainsteering workshop, built around questions that were specifically designed to find ideas for reducing the cost of insuring the car.

At first most of the ideas were not very original—people simply focused on ways to improve the safety of the car. Why were the ideas mediocre? Because CarCo had already focused on safety for decades—and remember, the Innovation S-curve predicts that when examining familiar areas, it takes more and more mental effort to produce fewer and fewer new ideas.

Fortunately, one question did soon produce a *very* new idea. An idea for a whole new business—and a whole new source of revenue—for CarCo. That question was: "What can we, as a *car* company, know that an *insurance* company can't?" After a few unproductive minutes spent discussing the sales and financing process, the client team narrowed its focus to the driver's actual operation of the car itself. The insight came instantly: "We can know *everything*—it's all right there in the engine management chip."

You see, every car built in the last few years is monitored and controlled by a series of onboard computers that measure everything from the car's speed, to its acceleration, to the spinning of the wheels. Furthermore, modern GPS systems can match that data with the exact location of the car at an exact point in time. And a device equivalent to a built-in cell phone could easily upload all that data to an insurance company's headquarters for analysis.

The result? A new business—call it "CarCo Insurance Company"—that would sell each driver an insurance policy for which the premiums would be based on how he actually drives the car each day, rather than simply on his age, the previous accidents he's been in, or the number of parking tickets he's gotten. The computers could know if he speeds down back streets, skids around corners, fails to put his blinker on, drives at high speed when there's snow or ice on the ground, and every other behavior necessary to provide perfectly individualized underwriting. And best of all, the policy would be completely nondiscriminatory: "Your premium is based on how *you* drive, not how other young single males drive. And you can affect your own premiums in real time. Need to lower your premium next month? Then drive like an angel instead of a NASCAR wannabe."

This particular idea is a killer. After all, the invention would turn traditional insurance companies' own processes against them. They typically charge premiums for a particular group of drivers that they insure (such as young single males) based on the average losses incurred by those drivers. But ask yourself: "Which young single male drivers should prefer CarCo's new type of policy, and which ones should prefer the old?" The answer is clear: Those who drive more carefully than average should leave their traditional insurer and migrate to CarCo Insurance Company, while the ones who drive less carefully than average should stick with traditional insurers. That means the average loss experience of—and the cost of associated payouts by—the traditional insurance companies will get worse and worse over time, making them even less able to compete with CarCo Insurance Company.

Now, this isn't an idea that can come to market overnight in its ultimate form. It'll take many years to build the databases and experience required to statistically link the full range of potential new risk factors to actual accident experience and set individual drivers' rates accordingly. But leading companies are already beginning to pursue crude early versions of this idea: for example, Progressive Insurance currently offers a product called Snapshot that allows customers to earn discounts based on a small subset of the risk factors that could ultimately be tracked in the future. Once insurance companies begin offering more sophisticated, fully realized versions of this idea, the results will be revolutionary.

RAMP UP THE INTENSITY OF YOUR QUESTIONS

Most Right Questions can be phrased in "soft" ways or "hard" ways. For a Billion-Dollar idea, you need to phrase it in a "hard" way—a way that forces your thinkers to look for major departures from current practices, significant exceptions versus average consumer needs, glaring differences in costs, and so on.

Don't just ask, "What stops some people who like our product from buying it?" Instead, ask, "What group of potential customers is as large as our entire current customer base but isn't buying our product for one particular reason?" That's the kind of question that can lead to guitars for girls (Daisy Rock Guitars), makeup for men (men already spend over $1 billion on grooming products each year in the United States, and 40 percent of European men buy skin-care products such as moisturizers), and even (as you'll recall from Chapter 2) sweet potato washing machines in China.[10]

Similarly, don't just ask "How can we expand distribution to meet our 5 percent volume growth objective this year?" Instead, ask "What would it take to get our product within arm's reach of every consumer on the planet?" That's actually been the distribution objective of The Coca-Cola Company for decades. In fact, here's a telling indicator of Coke's perennially aggressive mind-set.

It's early 1998, and Coke executives are preparing to release the company's 1997 Annual Report to Shareholders. The company is about to mark a milestone: by the time shareholders receive their copy of the annual report, sales of Coca-Cola beverage products will exceed 1 billion servings per day worldwide. But Wall Street analysts and investors are starting to wonder: "Can Coke possibly continue to deliver significant incremental volume growth in the years ahead? Haven't their beverages [sorry, we can't resist] saturated the market by now?"

When the annual report is released, the cover is almost entirely white. It features a simple graphic showing forty-eight of Coke's iconic contour bottles, arranged neatly into six rows of eight bottles each. Forty-seven of the bottles are shown merely as white embossed silhouettes against the white background of the cover. Way down in the bottom right-hand corner, a single lonely bottle, colored in red, accompanies a tiny, three-word headline: "One Billion Down." When the reader opens the cover, the image on the inside of the cover is completely reversed: the colors of the bottles are now flipped, and amidst what is now a virtual sea of red bottles, a single white bottle stands beside another tiny headline: "47 Billion to Go." On the facing page are two simple sentences: "This year, even as we sell 1 billion servings of our products daily, the world will still consume 47 billion servings of other beverages *every day*. We're just getting started."[11]

Don't just ask, "How can we cut costs by 10 percent?" Instead, ask "How can we cut costs by 30 percent and still meet the needs of at least 25 percent of the market?" Remember Dell and Jiffy Lube?

Here's an opportunity that still exists today—but be warned, capturing it will require you to answer a *very* intense question. Consider eyeglasses. Invented in the late thirteenth century, eyeglasses regularly appear on short lists of the most important inventions of the last 1,000—or even 2,000—years. A 1999 *Newsweek* article quoted Nicholas Humphrey of the New School for Social Research as saying, "[Eyeglasses] have effectively doubled the active life of everyone who reads or does fine work."[12] But even 800 years after their invention, eyeglasses are not available to the majority of the world's population. Why not? In a word: cost. According to the World Bank, in 2005 just under 50 percent of the world's population lived on less than $2.00 per day.[13] But the cost of eyeglasses in the developing world has been estimated by one source at $40 to $60 a pair.[14]

So a Billion-Dollar Question might be "How can eyeglasses be made and distributed for less than one-tenth of their current cost?" A small nonprofit company has been established to do just that. Vision-Spring has found ways to design and source their glasses, and to bypass expensive distribution channels, that enable them to sell eyeglasses on a small scale in the developing world for approximately $4.00 per pair. But the market is still wide open for even better solutions.

BE ABSOLUTELY RUTHLESS IN YOUR EVALUATION

How can you know whether a new idea that's passed the normal tests for *good* is actually *great*? First, establish tough, objective standards before you begin searching for ideas, and then ensure that you and others evaluate the ideas ruthlessly against those standards. The most common mistake is to leave the standard-setting until after you've found your pet idea. This is clearly a fundamentally flawed procedure, if for no other reason than because the nature of your standards will most likely be designed to measure how much better the new product is on the attribute that you've already decided is most important, rather than on the attribute the customer thinks is most important.

Second, find a tough benchmark to compare your results to. In our Z–1–4 project at McKinsey, we asked whether there were any common standards that various companies all seemed to reach and that drove their success. (Remember that forty-two out of the forty-three Z–1–4 companies approached or reached the billion-dollar revenue mark based on a single idea.) Here's what we found: with the exception of DreamWorks SKG (the forty-third company, which was based on a combination of animation, movies, and recordings) and L.A. Gear (whose rise was tied to a fashion trend), all of the Z–1–4 companies could be divided into three groups:

COMPANIES THAT OFFERED DRAMATICALLY LOWER PRICES

This group includes such icons as Dell, Amazon, Staples, and Price-line.com. The value proposition was "comparable quality at a far lower price." How much lower? The minimum amount was 20 percent, and average was over 30 percent. Their key innovation, of course, was not the price cut per se (although that was what drove the customers in the door), it was whatever innovation enabled them to cut their prices so much and still make a healthy profit at the same time.

COMPANIES THAT ACHIEVED AT LEAST A THREE-YEAR JUMP ON ALL THEIR INDUSTRY COMPETITORS ON ONE OF THE TOP THREE BUYING FACTORS FOR THEIR CATEGORY OF PRODUCT

The performance of every category of product improves over time. Therefore, at any point, one company's product might perform a little better than its competitors' products on the category's key buying factors. Then a few months later, another company's product might jump ahead by a little, and so on. After a while, customers (perhaps without even knowing it) come to expect a certain rate of improvement. Mostly, this rate of improvement is very steady. Innovations come every three or four months, and any one innovation improves the performance by three or four months' worth.

This category of Z–1–4 companies, including Home Depot, Iomega Zip Drive, and others, broke the mold by introducing a product or service that, instead of representing a few months' worth of improvement, represented at least three years' worth. In Home Depot's case, that meant offering (in addition to lower prices) ten times the number of SKUs found in traditional hardware stores. In Iomega's case, it meant offering seventy times the storage space of the then-standard product, floppy disks.

COMPANIES THAT "REINVENTED" AN ENTIRE CATEGORY BY EXCELLING AT AN ATTRIBUTE THAT HAD NOT PREVIOUSLY BEEN RECOGNIZED AS BEING IMPORTANT, BUT THAT INSTANTLY BECAME ONE OF THE TOP THREE BUYING FACTORS FOR A LARGE SEGMENT OF THE MARKET

Take Compaq. Their genius was to recognize that a significant portion of the early adopters of personal computers were salespeople, consultants, accountants, and other businesspeople whose jobs involved travel. At the time, industry magazines devoted to the personal computer market compared new machines based primarily on speed, memory, and cost, and those attributes dominated the attention of most computer makers. But the three engineers who founded Compaq recognized that *portability* was a crucial attribute for the sizable customer segment of traveling businesspeople.

In a similar way, megasuccessful pharmaceutical company Amgen rose to prominence by introducing a new product, Epogen, that helped kidney dialysis patients significantly—not necessarily by improving the efficacy of the dialysis itself, but by dramatically reducing one of its most frequent and highly undesirable side effects: constant nausea.

One more? eBay didn't try to become a better online store. Nor did it try to simply bring online a marketplace that already existed, such as a stock market. Instead, eBay created an entirely new marketplace for buyers and sellers of small, inexpensive items, who were scattered across the country and could never have found each other any other way.

Well, as they say in Hollywood, "That's a wrap." We hope you've enjoyed yourself, and that we've taught you a few helpful tricks along the way.

In particular, we hope we've helped you to thoroughly understand why, and how, you should ask the Right Questions, enabling you to identify all kinds of powerful new ideas that might never have occurred to you in the past. We hope we've shown you how to maximize your personal ideation skills, both by systematically exploring every possible nook and cranny of an issue to find new ideas, and by systematically evaluating and honing your ideas as you go. Finally, we hope we've enabled you to confidently and effectively lead others in the development of new ideas, whether once or on an ongoing basis.

And in the end, we hope we've changed forever the way you think about new ideas, by steering your creativity (don't be modest—you knew you had it in you!) in a productive new direction.

So get out there, ask the Right Questions, and make us proud. And if this book leads you to a Billion-Dollar Idea, you owe us a ride on your private jet.

Appendix

101 Right Questions to Spur Breakthrough Ideas

Right Questions are ones that make you take a different perspective on your problem than any you've taken before.

The questions below aren't intended to be a comprehensive list of all the Right Questions that can be asked—you know from reading this book that a truly comprehensive list would be virtually infinite—but they *are* intended to spur your thinking by exposing you to a number of perspectives that our clients have found fresh and useful. All have proved powerful in a wide range of settings.

We hope you'll recognize many of these questions from earlier chapters; others we didn't have room to discuss in this book—but if there's a sequel . . .

RIGHT QUESTIONS FOR NEW PRODUCTS AND SERVICES

Unsolved Customer Problems

- What's the biggest (avoidable) hassle that customers have to put up with?
- For which users, or which uses, or which occasions, are current products least well suited?

- For which subset of users are the processes and procedures associated with using our product least well suited?
- What are the major recent changes in rules or regulations that affect our suppliers or customers, but that we assumed would not change how we serve them?
- Who has a significant need for this product but is prevented from buying (or using) it because of one obstacle?
- Who doesn't use our product because it's inaccessible at certain times or places?
- Who doesn't use our product because there is something objectionable about it, or about the process of using it?
- What unpleasant side effects are associated with our product (or its components)?
- What is objectionable about the process of purchasing our product (or its competitors)?
- Who doesn't understand how to use our product?
- Who doesn't use our product because special ability is required?
- For whom does our product take too long to use?
- Who can't use our product due to some physical limitation (of time, of space, of distance, of the user, and so on) or some other innate characteristic?
- What is common to the twenty most frequent or most vociferous complainers who call into our customer service lines?

De-Averaging Users and Activities
- Who uses our product/service in surprisingly large quantities (and why, and what can we do about that)?
- Which customers does our industry prefer not to serve?
- Which customers don't need the full set of capabilities that we charge our customers for?
- Where have changes in the competitive landscape left some customers poorly served relative to the past?

- Do any of our customers need vastly more or less sales and service attention than most?
- For which customers are our support costs (such as order entry, tracking, customer-specific design) either unusually high or unusually low?
- Who spends at least 50 percent of what our product costs to adapt it to their specific needs?
- Could we still meet the needs of a significant subset of customers if we stripped out 25 percent of the hard or soft costs from our product?
- Which customers' needs are shifting most rapidly? What will they be in five years?
- Who is using our product under extreme conditions?
- Is there a humdrum portion of our work mix that is so routine it could become a low-cost stand-alone business?
- Who already spends twice as much (or more) for a competitor's variant of our product due to some particular feature, function, or tailoring? How can this become the norm?
- Which group of potential customers that we originally believed would be major purchasers of our product before it was introduced has, in fact, bought only a disappointing amount of our product? Why?

Exploring Unexpected Successes

- Who uses our product/service in ways we never expected or intended?
- Which customers purchase our product in the most unusual way by using an unexpected channel or process?
- Who has modified our product most extensively after purchasing it?
- Who is adapting/disassembling our product to use only a key component (or conversely, who is combining it with other products in a unique way)?

- What information do we generate in the process of conducting our business that could be used in radically different ways or in another business?
- Who would value information about our customers?
- Who is our single most successful salesperson, and what does he/ she say about our product that's different from what an average salesperson says? What does that tell us about our product's *real* benefits?

Imagining Perfection

- Who (or what) "does our thing" best in all the world, and how could we adapt their practices to our circumstances?
- For what subset of users can our product or service be an absolutely perfect solution?
- How would I do this if I weren't constrained by . . . ?
- How would we do things differently if we had perfect (or at least much better) information about our buyers, their usage, our distribution channels, and so on?
- What would we do differently if we could trust our customers not to cheat us (or didn't care that only a few did)?
- How would our product change if it were tailored for every customer?

Discovering Unrecognized Headroom

- Where do the "rules" already provide more flexibility than we (or others) currently take advantage of?
- Where are we operating under a set of rules that we've accepted for a long time without ever going back and reexamining what they actually say?
- Which technologies embedded in our product have changed the most since the product was last redesigned?
- Which technologies underlying our production and operating

processes have changed the most since we last redesigned our product or rebuilt our manufacturing and distribution systems?

Other Great Questions

- What do Rollerblades, Häagen-Dazs ice cream, and the *Batman* movies have in common?
- What group of potential customers is as large as our current customer base, but aren't customers for one particular reason?
- What other items or activities are highly related to our current product, and are ones that our product could be modified to take advantage of?
- What information about customers and product use is created as a by-product of our business that could be the key to radically improving the economics of another business?
- Who else deals with the same generic problem that we do, but for an entirely different reason (and how have they addressed it)?
- What other products are out there that actually derive from customers using our product and that cost at least as much as our product?
- What major breakthroughs in efficiency or effectiveness have we made in our business that could be applied in another business or country, and how can we gain directly from our greater expertise?

RIGHT QUESTIONS FOR MORE SUCCESSFUL SELLING EFFORTS

- Who is our single most successful salesperson, and how does he or she behave differently from our average salesperson? How does he find prospects? Which of our product's features does she emphasize? How does he describe our product's benefits? What does she do to follow up after the initial sales call? How should our other salespeople change their behavior accordingly?
- What currently distinguishes our top five referral sources from our bottom five?

- What market that we don't currently serve is the literal or virtual "hometown" of a critical mass of our salespeople and managers?
- What information do we not collect in the selling process (or do we collect but not use in the design process) that could make better products for certain segments of customers?
- Which applicants for our sales positions are turned down due to missing data, rather than a fully vetted bad score? How could we efficiently obtain the data on some of them?
- What would be the signs that a particular customer has fully considered our product and simply decided not to buy, so that we'll know when to quit expending selling efforts?

RIGHT QUESTIONS FOR REDUCING COSTS
All Departments

- What complexity do we plan for every day that, if eliminated, could change the way we operate?
- What can we do to consolidate or restructure the jobs of any less than fully busy people?
- Where do we have employees whose jobs consist of one part that is less pleasant but more valuable to the company, and another that is more pleasant but less valuable? How can we move 25 percent more of their attention toward the former and away from the latter?
- If we assumed we should be able to reduce the number of hours devoted to supervision by about 10 percent in each year that the duties of a given department remain largely unchanged (and so long as there has been little turnover), which departments could have their supervisors' spans of control widened?
- How is our workload shaped by the existence of other groups outside our department? Do their arbitrary deadlines and requirements unnecessarily increase our workload?
- Where is there a large disparity between the cost of handling the

routine first 90 percent of the items we deal with, and the cost of handling the exceptional last 10 percent? What would it take to eliminate the exceptional items?

- Could we save money if we could shift the time of day, week, or month that we undertake certain tasks? (For example, how could we shift the work to times when the rest of our department is slow? Could the work be done more efficiently in batches? Is there a real penalty to being available online for fewer hours of the day? Could the work be done more efficiently if it was not done on a first in, first out basis?)
- Where do we currently spend resources just in case events might occur? Are those events ones that haven't actually occurred in the last five years? If they do occur in the future, might they be a little embarrassing but not actually very costly?
- Are there situations in which we could reduce costs in our department if Department X would change what it's doing, but they can't currently change because they are budget constrained?
- Where has the pattern of use changed since we built our facilities and designed our programs, in ways that would enable us to reduce the resources devoted to less important activities?

Administrative Expenses

- What would have to happen to remove all staff support of a particular kind or in a particular location?
- In what areas is the efficiency of a department "trapped" by outdated restrictions placed on it by company policies?
- Where do we still use people to process routine forms or information, rather than have it done electronically without human intervention?
- Are our needs really so unique that we should ignore the potential benefits of outsourcing payroll, benefits management, recruiting, media planning, and so on?
- Do we prepare long reports with comprehensive data when only

exceptions matter, or where the true consequences of variances are quite small?

- Do we prepare reports that cover short periods of time and/or are delivered in real time, when longer periods and/or slower reporting would meet the need just as well?
- How have business requirements shifted since we last fundamentally redesigned any one of our administrative processes? Has the need for certain data or certain analyses become significantly lower or even disappeared altogether?
- Do our various staff departments conduct ad hoc analysis only if there is an explicit hypothesis about what the analysis will prove and an up-front agreement regarding which decisions should change, in which ways, if the hypothesis proves correct? Or do they spend significant time conducting random analyses hoping to "find something interesting" in the data? If the latter, what is their track record?
- Do we have multiple departments (such as marketing, sales, manufacturing, finance) reprocessing and repackaging the same data, or multiple departments analyzing the same event from multiple angles? Can that be made more efficient?
- Which of our electronic storage, retrieval, and software policies (such as type and amount of content saved; real-time access versus near-real-time access versus delayed retrieval; versions of software supported) could be modified to produce significant reductions in capital and/or operating expenses?

Purchasing and Distribution Expenses

- What would it take to be able to bypass the least efficient part of our supply or distribution chain?
- Where do our practices place an unnecessary burden on others around the company? How could we share the gains if we changed our own requirements?
- What kinds of supplies and services (such as local travel) are

bought in small, independent batches across the company and over time, that could be bought less expensively via aggregation and greater coordination?

Customer-Driven Expenses
- What small percentage of our customers takes up a large percentage of our time and cause us hassle?
- What activities might our customers prefer to do for themselves if only they could?
- Which products/services/activities are expensive to produce/support and appeal to only a small set of customers?

Other Great Questions
- What could we do differently if everyone had a certain level of education?
- How can the skill component in our processes be decreased dramatically?
- If we were to redesign every offering and management process from scratch to meet today's needs and using today's technology, what would we change the most?
- What additional steps in process or information could be required as part of the selling process that could reduce accounts receivable write-offs later?
- Which locations, facilities, machines, etc. (or portions thereof) are highly maintained but used only rarely?
- What mishaps/incidents cause expensive repairs to happen most frequently during a typical year, and what can be done to reduce the frequency and/or repair costs of such events?
- Where are we furthest from the "efficient frontier" of zero excess use of utilities, zero excess capacity, most efficient time of day, and absolute least cost provider? How might we use time-, place-, and resource-shifting to improve our efficiency?
- What "indirect spending" is done by our key suppliers and

customers that is ancillary to working with us, for which we can either be the vendor or aggregate those purchases in return for a fee received from the vendor?

- What entities benefit economically to the greatest extent from our presence, and what could they do to help us succeed?
- Where do we have underutilized resources (such as low overall utilization; day- or season-specific utilization of facilities, staffers, or other assets) that are not really important to how we compete, but are similar to underutilized resources of competitors, and that we could share?

And as long as we're on the subject of Right Questions, here's a list that many people (clients and nonclients alike) have told us they found helpful in solving an age-old problem that they face in their personal lives many times each year:

RIGHT QUESTIONS FOR FINDING THE PERFECT GIFT

- What was the intended recipient's favorite toy, hobby, or activity during the period of their life that they look back on most fondly?
- What event or accomplishment are they most proud of in their life?
- What place, person, or group of people were they once very fond of, but have since lost touch with?
- What would be the ultimate experience associated with their hobby or interest, and how could they have that experience (or a proxy for it)?
- Has there recently been a new invention that dramatically changes how well they can perform an important aspect of their hobby, or even their daily routine?
- What is the perfect gift that *only* they could give you, and what does that tell you about the perfect gift that only you could give them?

- What do you do better than most people but have never used to create a gift before?
- What are the gifts that you've seen make the biggest emotional impact on the recipient, and what was the question that could have led the giver to think of them?

Acknowledgments

Brainsteering: *A Better Approach to Breakthrough Ideas* represents the codification of a body of knowledge and the lessons of practice gathered over the past fourteen years. Along the way, literally hundreds of people have contributed to the development of the Brainsteering approach in ways large and small, from colleagues who spent months of their careers researching key points to clients who spent a few hours serving as "test subjects" for each of its helpful innovations (as well as many unhelpful innovations that were tested and dropped along the way).

We sincerely thank everyone who supported us on this journey. Although space constraints prevent us from naming each person individually, there are several people to whom we are particularly indebted, and to whom we'd like to offer these acknowledgements as a small token of our gratitude.

First, we'd like to thank the current and former partners of McKinsey & Company. They mentored us from the earliest days of our careers, gave us opportunities to focus on the subjects of this book, and underwrote multiple projects that laid the intellectual foundations upon which we built our ideas, both during and after our time with the firm. Further, they generously allowed us to share that knowledge with you here. Lenny Mendonca, Dominic Barton, Rajat Gupta, Ian Davis, Somu Subramaniam, and Bill Barnett particularly stand out in our minds.

Second, we'd like to thank our colleagues at McKinsey for their many valuable contributions. The concept of finding breakthrough ideas by asking the right questions emerged from the Killer Ideas sub-team of the McKinsey Strategy Theory Initiative. The concept first emerged in discussions with Michelle Horn. Renee Dye was instrumental in its first full articulation. Trish Clifford brought academic rigor to our thought processes. Trish and Renee ran dozens of early workshops, improving our processes and techniques every time. They and Cyriac Roeding developed our first formal workshop guides and compiled the first extensive lists of Right Questions and signpost examples. The Z–1–4 (zero to $1 billion within 4 years) project was co-led by Eberhard von Lohneysen, who was a great and inspiring leader. Alex Reznikovich, Gennady Gazin, Lev Nicolau, and Trey Loughran managed the work, drawing unexpected insights from a mountain of research conducted by a small army of more than twenty consultants.

We also thank Dick Foster for all of his encouragement over the years and for his many intellectual contributions to the field of innovation, which helped us sharpen our understanding regarding the nature of new ideas and how they emerge.

Beyond McKinsey, special thanks go to the editors of the *Harvard Business Review*, especially Tom Stewart, Sarah Cliffe, and Steve Prokesch, for first publishing many of the ideas underlying the Brain-steering approach ("Breakthrough Thinking from Inside the Box," *Harvard Business Review*, December 2007).

Over the past three years, as we expanded and refined the Brain-steering approach and began to create this book, another group of indispensable individuals played key roles. Our father, Edward Coyne Sr., encouraged us, conducted research for us, and read our unpolished drafts more often than anyone else on the planet. Jan Thrapp tirelessly researched everything from obscure articles in social psychology journals to stories of celebrity misconduct in gossip magazines. We thank them both for their diligence, their patience, and their constant good spirits.

Eric Lupfer, our agent at WME Entertainment, taught us how to craft a book that could actually be worth publishing, and generated more enthusiasm from publishers than we had any right to expect.

And finally, Hollis Heimbouch, our editor and publisher at Harper-Collins, worked her magic as only she can to make our material more useful, more interesting, and more accessible to our readers—who, we hope, will enjoy reading this book as much as we enjoyed writing it.

A Note on Sources

Many of the concepts, principles, techniques, examples, and analyses described in this book are based upon our own personal life experience and/or our past consulting experience at McKinsey & Company, The Coyne Partnership, and other firms where we have had the pleasure of working with, and for, a variety of outstanding individuals and organizations in both the private and public sectors. In some cases, additional details beyond those cited in this book are not available for public disclosure for reasons ranging from personal privacy to client confidentiality. However, many other of the concepts, principles, techniques, examples, and analyses described here reflect information we have obtained through the published work of others, and/or through personal interviews with individuals who have generously allowed us to cite them by name. In such cases, we offer our deepest thanks to each of the individuals, publications, and organizations cited in the notes that follow, for providing us with information that proved highly useful in creating this book.

NOTES

Introduction: Why Brainsteering?

1. Mari Attoun, "Cornfield Craze," americanprofile.com, August 20, 2006, www.americanprofile.com/article/5487.html.

2. Don Frantz interview by Kevin P. Coyne and Shawn T. Coyne, February 16, 2010.

3. Sources for visitor statistics for the Grand Canyon, "Top 25 Most Visited Tourist Destinations in America," *TheTravelersZone.com*, March 10, 2008, www.thetravelerszone.com/travel-destinations/top-25-most-visited-tourist-destinations-in-america (accessed March 16, 2010); for the Statue of Liberty, Michael Saul, "Statue of Liberty Crown to Reopen July 4," *U.S. News & World Report*, May 8, 2009, www.usnews.com/news/national/articles/2009/05/08/statue-of-liberty-crown-to-reopen-july-4.html; for Mount Rushmore, Andrea J. Cook, "Without Rushmore Fireworks, Tourism Loses Thousands in Free Advertising," *Rapid City Journal*, January 15, 2010, www.rapidcityjournal.com/news/article_512d4cc6-018c-11df-835a-001cc4c002e0.html; and for Mardi Gras, Jennifer Hale, "Mardi Gras 2010 Turning into Huge Milestone," *Fox8Live.com*, February 17, 2010, www.fox8live.com/mostpopular/story/Mardi-Gras-2010-turning-into-huge-milestone/Ode0Cw0K-0G6-ZPaGqjD4w.cspx.

4. Frantz interview.

5. "Compaq: From Place Mat Sketch to PC Giant," *USA Today*, September 4, 2001, www.usatoday.com/tech/techinvestor/2001-09-04-compaq-history.htm.

6. Alan M. Webber, "Consensus, Continuity, and Common Sense: An Interview with Compaq's Rod Canion," *Harvard Business Review* 68, no.4 (July/August 1990): 115.

7. "The History of Wicked," http://wickedthemusical.com.au/about/history.html (accessed March 17, 2010).

8. Ibid.

9. "UFC Tickets," *showtimetickets.com*, www.showtimetickets.com/sports/fighting/ ufc.jsp (accessed March 24, 2010).

10. Ibid.

11. Fulton Shelley, "Fighting for Higher Ground: American Fight League Battles to Change Mixed Martial Arts' Image," *Sunday Paper*, May 25, 2008, www .sundaypaper.com/More/Archives/tabid/98/articleType/ArticleView/articleId/ 2449/Fighting-for-higher-ground.aspx (accessed June 11, 2010).

12. Kevin Lole, "Carwin's Star Rises as UFC 106 Nears," *Yahoo! Sports*, September 3, 2009, http://sports.yahoo.com/mma/news?slug=ki-carwin090209.

13. A. F. Osborn, *Applied Imagination: Principles and Procedures of Creative Problem-Solving* (New York: Charles Scribner's Sons, 1957), 80–84.

14. For two particularly useful academic studies on the ineffectiveness and inefficiency of traditional brainstorming, see Paul A. Mongeau, "The Brainstorming Myth" (paper presented at the Annual Meeting of the Western States Communication Association, Albuquerque, N.M., February 15, 1993), 1–26, www .eric.ed.gov/ERICDocs/data/ericdocs2sql/content_storage_01/0000019b/80/13/ c5/0f.pdf (accessed March 24, 2010); and Fredric M. Jablin and David R. Seibold, "Implications for Problem Solving Groups of Empirical Research on 'Brainstorming': A Critical Review of the Literature," *Southern Speech Communication Journal* 48 (Summer 1978): 328–29.

Chapter 1: The Proven Power of Questions to Help You Find Ideas

1. "Profile: Tito the Spaceman," *BBC News*, April 28, 2001, http://news.bbc.co.uk/ 2/hi/science/nature/1297924.stm.

2. Alistair M. Hanna and Jerrold T. Lundquist, "Creative Strategies," *McKinsey Quarterly* 3 (1990): 56.

3. Fred Sauceman, "Once Tiny, National Gingerbread House Competition Now a Giant," *GoTricities.com*, cached January 26, 2010.

4. "Grove Park Inn National Gingerbread House Competition," *romanticasheville .com*, www.romanticasheville.com/gingerbread.htm (accessed March 17, 2010).

5. Sources for Jiffy Lube store count statistics: for store count at time of sale to Pennzoil, Merry Sheils, "W. James Hindman—Youth Services International Chief Executive Officer—N.B.," *Chief Executive*, September 1994, http://find articles.com/p/articles/mi_m4070/is_n97/ai_16320052/?tag=content;col1; and for current store count, "Jiffy Lube: History & Mission," www.jiffylube.com/ about/historyandmission.aspx (accessed October 14, 2009).

6. Jeanne Ridgway, "Jiffy Lube Co-Founder: Great Ideas Need Action," South Jersey *Courier Post*, November 19, 2008, www.rowan.edu/colleges/business/cie/ documents/Spinelliarticle111908.pdf.

7. Jeffry A. Timmons and Stephen Spinelli, *New Venture Creation: Entrepreneurship for the 21st Century*, 6th edition (Boston: McGraw-Hill/Irwin, 2004), 491.

Chapter 2: Developing Your Arsenal of Right Questions

1. Richard N. Foster, *Innovation: The Attacker's Advantage* (New York: Summit Books, 1986), 31.

2. Andrew Stone, "How I Made It: Trevor Baylis, Inventor of the Clockwork Radio," *Sunday Times*, May 22, 2005, http://business.timesonline.co.uk/tol/business/entrepreneur/article524972.ece.

3. Source for sales of Freeplay radios, Stone, "How I Made It"; and for honorary degrees and personal accolades bestowed upon Baylis, "Trevor Baylis OBE—Our President," *trevorbaylisbrands.com*, www.trevorbaylisbrands.com/tbb/aboutus/trevorbaylis/trevor.asp (accessed March 17, 2010).

4. "King of the Mountain Bike," (interview of Mike Sinyard by Maggie Overfelt) *CNNmoney.com*, May 16, 2008, http://money.cnn.com/2008/05/15/smbusiness/specialized_bikes.fsb/index.htm.

5. Chester Dawson. "No Kidding—A New Market for Baby Food: Manufacturers Are Targeting Japan's Elderly Population," *Business Week Online*, January 27, 2003, www.businessweek.com/magazine/content/03_04/b3817161.htm.

6. "Church & Dwight Co., Inc. 2008 Annual Report," *churchdwight.com*, April 8, 2009, http://media.corporate-ir.net/media_files/irol/11/110737/reports/ar08/HTML2/church_dwight-ar2008_0013.htm.

7. Lisa Bonnema, "International Appliance Technical Conference 2004 IATC—A New Perspective," May 2004, www.appliancemagazine.com/editorial.php?article=498.

8. "Haier Management Trilogy: A System with the Combination of Corporate Culture," *International Hometex.Net*, October 7, 2008, www.fzpzw.cn/InfoContent/&id=10331878-cdb8-48db-9b7c-ce0acfe94ac7&comp_stats=compFrontInfo_listMultiPage-001.html (accessed June 11, 2010).

9. David Berkoff interview by Kevin P. Coyne and Shawn T. Coyne, February 22, 2010.

10. Michael L. Kasavana, "V-Commerce: Understanding Vending Machine Technology," *hospitality.net*, April 19, 2002, www.hospitalitynet.org/news/4011592.search?query=wireless+technology+and+vending+machines.

11. Robert F. McDermott and Thomas A. Teal, "Service Comes First: An Interview with USAA's Robert F. McDermott," *Harvard Business Review* 69, no. 5 (September/October 1991): 116–26.

12. "Self Checkout," *Wikipedia*, http://en.wikipedia.org/wiki/Self_checkout (accessed February 2, 2010).

13. David Fleming, "Shock to the System," *ESPN.com*, December 18, 2008, http://sports.espn.go.com/espn/print?id=3779821.

14. Mitch Stephens, "Bay Area Confidential: Piedmont's A-11 is A-OK," *Maxpreps.com*, republished on *The Piedmont A–11 Offense Blog*, November 19, 2007, http://a11offense.blogspot.com.

15. Steve Humphries interview by Shawn T. Coyne, February 23, 2010.

16. Fleming, "Shock to the System."

17. Ibid.

Chapter 3: When It's Time to Find a Better Idea

1. "Dell," *Wikipedia,* http://en.wikipedia.org/wiki/Dell (accessed February 2, 2010).
2. Anand Giridharadas, "Four Wheels for the Masses: The $2,500 Car," *New York Times,* January 8, 2008, www.nytimes.com/2008/01/08/business/worldbusiness/08indiacar.html.
3. "Tata Nano Review," *cardekho.com,* www.cardekho.com/carmodels/Tata/Tata_Nano (accessed March 24, 2010).
4. "Review of Tata Nano," *techwebtoday.com,* http://techwebtoday.com/review/tata-nano.html (accessed March 24, 2010).
5. "First Nano Owner Gets Keys to Car," *BBC News,* July 17, 2009, http://news.bbc.co.uk/2/hi/south_asia/8155332.stm.
6. Ibid.

Chapter 5: The Right (and Wrong) Uses of Analysis in Ideation

1. For further information regarding FedEx's $200 million in ZapMail-related operating losses, see "Federal Express Plans for ZapMail," *New York Times,* March 21, 1986, www.nytimes.com/1986/03/21/business/federal-express-plans-for-zapmail.html. For further information regarding its $320 million shutdown losses, see Calvin Sims, "Coast-to-Coast in 20 Seconds: Fax Machines Alter Business," *New York Times,* May 6, 1988, www.nytimes.com/1988/05/06/business/coast-to-coast-in-20-seconds-fax-machines-alter-business.html.
2. "Fractals Determine Date of Paintings," *Physicsworld.com,* June 4, 1999, http://physicsworld.com/cws/article/news/3028.
3. "Limited Brands—Victoria's Secret," *limitedbrands.com,* http://limited.com/brands/vs/vss/index.jsp (accessed June 11, 2010).
4. Michael Lewis, *Moneyball: The Art of Winning an Unfair Game* (New York: W. W. Norton, 2003). For further information regarding Oakland A's general manager Billy Beane, see "Baseball Operations: Billy Beane," *mlb.com,* http://mlb.mlb.com/oak/team/exec_bios/beane_billy.jsp (accessed March 18, 2010). For further information regarding Beane's early efforts to enable the Oakland A's to prosper as a smaller-market team, see Robert Hands, "Beane Throws a Curve-Ball into Arena of Management and Strikes Big Time," *Times (London),* July 11, 2003, www.timesonline.co.uk/tol/sport/article1149970.ece (accessed June 11, 2010).
5. Saul Hansell, "Some Hard Lessons for Online Grocer," *New York Times,* February 19, 2001, www.nytimes.com/2001/02/19/business/some-hard-lessons-for-online-grocer.html.
6. John T. Gourville, "Eager Sellers and Stony Buyers," *Harvard Business Review* 84, no. 6 (June 2006): 103.

Chapter 6: Optimizing Your Personal Ideation Performance

1. "AFL History—Attendance Charts," *Arenafan.com,* www.arenafan.com/history/?histleague=1&page=yearly&fpage=attendance (accessed March 18, 2010).

2. Shane Murphy, *The Achievement Zone* (New York: Penguin, 1996), 4.
3. F. Gregory Ashby, Alice M. Isen, and A.U. Turken, "A Neuropsychological Theory of Positive Affect and Its Influence on Cognition," *Psychological Review* 106, no. 3 (1999): 530, www.psych.ucsb.edu/~ashby/rev10635.pdf.
4. Carsten K. W. De Dreu, Matthijs Baas, and Bernard A. Nijstad, "Hedonic Tone and Activation Level in the Mood-Creativity Link: Toward a Dual Pathway to Creativity Model," *Journal of Personality and Social Psychology* 94, no. 5 (2008): 739–56, http://home.medewerker.uva.nl/c.k.w.dedreu/bestanden/DeDreu,%20 Nijstad%20et%20al.%20JPSP%202008.pdf.
5. Ibid.
6. Ibid.
7. Ibid.
8. Kathleen A. Martin Ginis and Steven R. Bray, "Application of the Limited Strength Model of Self-Regulation to Understanding Exercise Effort, Planning and Adherence," *Psychology and Health*, advance online publication, November 2009.
9. "Rough Day at Work? You Won't Feel Like Exercising," *McMaster University News Release*, September 24, 2009, www.mcmaster.ca/opr/html/opr/media/ main/NewsReleases/Exercisestudy.htm (accessed March 22, 2010).
10. Ibid.
11. Beth A. Hennessey, "The Social Psychology of Creativity," *Scandinavian Journal of Educational Research* 47, no. 3 (2003): 253, www.amshq.org/conference/ boston/handouts/00Hennessey.pdf (accessed March 11, 2010).
12. Ibid.
13. "Games People Play," *ericberne.com*, www.ericberne.com/Games_People_Play .htm (accessed March 18, 2010).

Chapter 8: Teaching Others to Develop Better Ideas

1. For four particularly well-known psychological studies examining the link between motivation and creativity, see E. L. Deci, "Effects of Externally-Mediated Rewards on Intrinsic Motivation," *Journal of Personality and Social Psychology* 18 (1971): 105–15; E. L. Deci and R. M. Ryan, *Intrinsic Motivation and Self-Determination in Human Behavior* (New York: Plenum, 1985); M. R. Lepper and D. Greene, eds., *The Hidden Costs of Reward* (Hillsdale, N.J.: Erlbaum, 1978); and M. R. Lepper, D. Greene, and R. E. Nisbett, "Undermining Children's Intrinsic Interest with Extrinsic Reward: A Test of the Overjustification Hypothesis," *Journal of Personality and Social Psychology* 28 (1978): 129–37.
2. Teresa M. Amabile, "Motivational Synergy: Toward New Conceptualizations of Intrinsic and Extrinsic Motivation in the Workplace," *Human Resource Management Review* 3, no. 3 (1993): 185–201.

Chapter 9: Creating an Idea Factory

1. Ben Silverman, "Guitar Hero III Becomes Top-Grossing Game Ever,"

videogames.yahoo.com, January 12, 2009, http://videogames.yahoo.com/printview_feature?eid=1278866.

2. Simon Carless, "Harmonix Talks *Guitar Hero*'s $1 Million Budget, *Guitar Freaks* Inspiration," *Gamasutra.com*, December 5, 2007, www.gamasutra.com/php-bin/news_index.php?story=16510.

3. Source for viewership and origin of cited television shows: For *American Idol* and *Dancing with the Stars*, "The Nielsen Company Issues Top Ten U.S. Lists for 2009," http://en-us.nielsen.com/etc/medialib/nielsen_dotcom/en_us/documents/pdf/press_releases/2009/december.Par.23739.File.dat/Nielsen%20Top%20Tens%202009%20final.pdf; for *Pop Idol*, "Pop Idol Mogul Sues Simon Cowell," *BBC News*, September 10, 2004, http://news.bbc.co.uk/2/hi/entertainment/3645004.stm; and for *Strictly Come Dancing*, "Strictly 'World's Most Watched,'" *BBC News*, November 10, 2008, http://news.bbc.co.uk/2/hi/entertainment/7719968.stm.

4. Richard Huff, "It's a Jackpot Year for ABC: 'Millionaire' Leads Network to Season Nielsen Crown," *New York Daily News*, May 24, 2000, www.nydailynews.com/archives/entertainment/2000/05/24/2000-05-24_it_s_a_jackpot_year_for_abc_.html (accessed June 11, 2010).

5. Source for viewership of *All in the Family*: "Bunker Mentality," *Entertainment-Weekly.com*, April 2, 1999, www.ew.com/ew/article/0,,272896,00.html; and for origin, "Lear, Norman," *The Museum of Broadcast Communications Online*, www.museum.tv/eotvsection.php?entrycode=learnorman (accessed March 18, 2010).

6. Source for production budget of original *Revenge of the Nerds*, "Revenge of the Nerds," *Wikipedia*, http://en.wikipedia.org/wiki/Revenge_of_the_Nerds (accessed February 2, 2010); for box office revenues of original movie, "Revenge of the Nerds," *boxofficemojo.com*, http://boxofficemojo.com/movies/?id=revengeofthenerds.htm (accessed March 17, 2010); and for box office revenues of sequel, "Revenge of the Nerds II: Nerds in Paradise," *boxofficemojo.com*, http://boxofficemojo.com/movies/?page=main&id=revengeofthenerds2.htm (accessed March 17, 2010).

7. "The Cutting Edge," *boxofficemojo.com*, http://boxofficemojo.com/movies/?id=cuttingedge.htm (accessed March 17, 2010).

8. "Bring It On," *boxofficemojo.com*, http://boxofficemojo.com/movies/?id=bringiton.htm (accessed March 17, 2010).

9. "Drumline," *boxofficemojo.com*, http://boxofficemojo.com/movies/?id=drumline.htm (accessed March 17, 2010).

10. "Stick It," *boxofficemojo.com*, www.boxofficemojo.com/movies/?id=stickit.htm (accessed March 17, 2010).

11. Statistics were compiled using *People* magazine, vol. 72, nos. 5, 10, 12, 13, 21, 22, 24, 25, and 26.

12. Sources for calculation of revenue growth of FedEx Express between 1998 and 2008: "FedEx Corporation Historical Statistics—FY 1998–FY 2007," *http://ir.fedex.com/annuals.cfm*, http://files.shareholder.com/downloads/

FDX/875740664x0x116104/FCCE51C6-B7CD-4A4D-805C-C035BEFC2F95/
historical_stat_book.pdf, page 11 (accessed March 24, 2010); and "FedEx
2009 Annual Report," *http://ir.fedex.com/annuals.cfm*, http://files.shareholder.
com/downloads/FDX/875740664x0x312397/557bd7f3-8372-4afe-a664-1fd
b82a488b0/FedEx2009AnnualReportl.pdf, page 18 (accessed March 24, 2010).

Chapter 10: Developing Your Own Billion-Dollar Idea

1. Gary Frenay, "Paul McCartney—We Believe in Yesterday," *pop-matters.com*, January 2, 2008, www.popmatters.com/pm/feature/
paul-mccartney-we-believe-in-yesterday.
2. Ibid.
3. Craig Cross, *The Beatles: Day-by-Day, Song-by-Song, Record-by-Record* (Lincoln, Neb.: iUniverse, 2005), 464–65.
4. Barry Miles, *Paul McCartney: Many Years from Now* (New York: Henry Holt & Company, 1997), 203.
5. The Beatles, *The Beatles Anthology* (San Francisco: Chronicle Books, 2000), 175.
6. Miles, *Paul McCartney*, 208.
7. Lev Grossman, "ALL TIME 100 Novels," *Time.com*, October 16, 2005, www
.time.com/time/specials/packages/article/0,28804,1951793_1951943_1952547,00.
html.
8. "Book," *lordoftheflies.org*, http://lordoftheflies.org/img/book.htm.
9. Robert Harris, "William Golding: The Man Who Wrote Lord of the Flies by John Carey" (book review), *Sunday Times*, August 30, 2009, http://entertainment
.timesonline.co.uk/tol/arts_and_entertainment/books/non-fiction/article
6811054.ece.
10. Rob Walker, "Consumed; Grooming for Guys," *New York Times*, July 25, 2004, www.nytimes.com/2004/07/25/magazine/the-way-we-live-now-7-25-04-consumed
-grooming-for-guys.html.
11. *Coca-Cola 1997 Annual Report*, Buckmaster Annual Stockholder Reports, http://
buck.com/annual_report?idx=C&co=KO&res=l&yr=97&nam=DEMO&pw=
DEMO.
12. Sharon Begley, "The Power of Big Ideas," *Newsweek*, January 11, 1999, www.newsweek.com/1999/01/10/the-power-of-big-ideas.html.
13. Shaohua Chen and Martin Ravallion, "The Developing World Is Poorer Than We Thought, but No Less Successful in the Fight Against Poverty," *Development Research Group, World Bank*, (August 16, 2008), 33, http://sit-eresources.worldbank.org/JAPANINJAPANESEEXT/Resources/515497-
1201490097949/080827_The_Developing_World_is_Poorer_than_we_
Thought.pdf.
14. "Business Model: Why Eyeglasses?" *Visionspring.org*, http://visionspring.org/
how-we-work/why-eyeglasses.php.

Index

academia: counterfactual history, 8

acting, 8

advertising agency, 158–59

institutional history, mining for ideas, 170

airline industry

airport priority access lines, 27

check-in kiosks, 27

hassle of airport experience and, 26–27

jet engines, 24

online check-in and boarding passes, 27, 37

private jets, 26, 37

All in the Family, 171

Amabile, Teresa, 161

Amazon, 6, 195

American Idol, 171

Amgen Epogen, 196–97

analysis in ideation, 85–112, 155, 156

art of Jackson Pollock, 89–90

creativity with, not exclusive of, 87–90, 113

databases and, 91

design on paper, 110

evaluating new ideas, 96–100

failure to analyze and business failure, 86–87, 97–100, 220n 1

first blush analysis: five issues, 102–7

four stages of, 101–11

looking for anomalies, 91, 92–96

matching stage of analysis to the development of the idea, 100–111

analysis in ideation (*cont.*)
  originating new ideas with,
    90–96
  quick discovery stage: four
    issues, 107–10
  sabermetrics in MLB, 92–94
  TV shows, 88–89
  two tendencies to avoid, 91–92
Annville, Pennsylvania, 2
Apple Computer, 4–5, 6
*Applied Imagination: Principles and
  Procedures of Creative Problem-
  Solving* (Osborn), 10
Arena Football League, 113
Arm & Hammer corporation,
  41–42
automobiles
  Brainsteering workshop to
    boost revenues, 190–92
  car space heaters, 38
  Ford Model T, 56
  India's "people's car," 55–56
  insurance innovation, 191–92
  Jiffy Lube idea, 28–30
  used car business, 26
Avatar, 174
Avenue Q, 19

baby food for seniors, 40
banking industry, 41
  credit card industry and Ci-
    tibank's innovation, 94–96
  subprime lending, 96

Batman films, 18–19, 37
Batten, Barton, Durstine &
  Osborn (BBDO), 10
Baylis, Trevor, 36
Beane, Billy, 93–94, 220n 4
Berkoff Blastoff, 44–45
Berkoff, David, 44–45
Berne, Eric, 129–30
bicycles, 37–38
Billion-Dollar Idea, 6, 12, 185–97
  automobile insurance innova-
    tion, 191–92
  evaluation, tough, objective,
    195–97
  eyeglasses, 194
  four principles, 185–86
  investment of time, finances,
    and frustration, 187–89
  large market as target, 190–92
  making a serious commitment,
    186–90
  ramping up intensity of Right
    Questions, 193–95
  sanity check in place, 189–90
  scale and nature of resources
    needed, 186–87
Brainsteering. *See also specific
  aspects of this approach*
  applications, business and
    personal, 2–3, 8–9, 12–13, 20,
    35–36
  brainstorming vs., 9–11, 133–
    36, 218n 14

creativity, innate, and, 3
finding the perfect gift, (example), 63–68
officially adopting in workplace, 169
optimizing your personal ideation performance, 113–30
origins of, 3–6
Right Process and, 4, 9–11
Right Question and, 4, 17–84 (*see also* Right Question)
sanity check, 35, 80–81, 189–90
teaching the approach to others, 155–57
two-part experiment, 17–21
Brainsteering sessions
conducting according to a strict formula, 145-46
length of sessions, 124–25, 145–46
number of Right Questions needed, 59–60
time between sessions, 125–26
Brainsteering workshops, 136–49
brainstorming vs., 133–36
creating subgroups, 141–42
feedback for participants about fate of ideas, 148–49
isolating "Idea Crushers," 141–42
orienting the participants, 143–44, 167

parlor tricks (including contests), 20, 144–45
post-workshop meeting with decision-makers, 148–49
preparation for, 137–42
running the workshop, 1 42–46
selecting participants for, 139–41
selecting the Right Questions for use during, 138–39
strict structure for group work, 145–46
summary of key principles and techniques, 136
understanding real-life constraints and criteria, 137–38
wrapping up, 146–48
brainstorming, 4, 9–11, 218n 14
bad brainstorming sessions, 133–34
costs of ineffective, 135–36
flawed methodology of, 134–35
ineffectiveness of, 9, 10–11, 17–18
worst aspect of, 145
Bring It On, 173–74
sequels, 174
Broadcast Music Incorporated (BMI), 187
Bryan, Kurt, 48–49
BusinessWeek.com, 40

Canion, Rod, 5

CarMax, 26

"category killer" stores, 7

Chia Pets, 104

Chinese washing machines, 42, 192

Chuck E. Cheese, 19

Church, Austin, 41

Cirque du Soleil, 19

Citibank, 95–96

Coca-Cola Company, 192–93

Commodore Computer, 7

Compaq Computer Corporation, 4–5, 6, 7, 17, 35, 54, 86, 186, 196

CompUSA, 7

Computer City, 7

consulting firms. *See also* McKinsey & Company

  databases of proprietary knowledge, 175

corn maze, 1–2

cost reduction ideas, 76–77, 77, 176, 204–8

  administrative expenses, 205–6

  all departments, 204–5

  customer-driven expenses, 207

  great questions, miscellaneous, 207–8

  production costs, 76–77, 77

  purchasing and distribution expenses, 206–7

Coyne Brothers' Principle of Preexisting Databases, 91

creativity

  analysis in ideation and, 87–90, 113

  applied, 89, 161

  emotions and, 114–20

  enhanced cognitive flexibility and, 116

  getting yourself in the zone, 114

  group ideation techniques, 133–49

  handling the "idea request from hell," 128–30

  idea factory, 165–81

  innate, and Brainsteering, 3

  motivation, intrinsic and extrinsic, 120–23, 221n 1

  neutralizing emotional overhead and, 117–20

  optimizing your personal ideation performance, 113–30

  physical environment, 123

  pure art, 89–90

  reusing the same questions and, 127–28

  right place, right time, 113

  role of a sounding board, 126–27

  tailoring the idea-generation process to your personal style, 123–28 teaching others, 151–64

unhealthy patterns, 31–34,
176–79

creativity, teaching, 151–64. *See
also* Brainsteering workshops

analysis of ideas, 155, 156

"controlled quality risks," 157

delegating appropriately,
157–59

establishing a baseline standard
of success, 152–55

four steps, 152

generating questions, 156

magazine group, content,
151–52

providing feedback, 160–64

television news, "nonbreaking"
stories, 153–55

using the Brainsteering approach in manageable steps,
155–57

using three skills of Brainsteering, 155–57

customer-focused Right Questions, 37–47, 199–203

de-averaging users and activities, 39–41, 200–201

exploring unexpected suc-
cesses, 41–43, 201–2

identifying unsolved customer
problems, 37–39, 199

imagining perfection, 43–47

what group of potential
customers . . . doesn't buy our
product or service, 38–39

what is the biggest hassle a customer has to deal with, 21–23,
25–27, 29, 37, 176, 199

what would we do differently if
we could trust our customers
not to cheat us, 46–47

what would we do differently
if we had perfect information
. . . , 45–46

which customers does our industry prefer not to serve, and
why, 40–41

for which users, on which occasions, are current products
least well suited, 37–38, 176,
200

who uses our product/service
in surprisingly large quantities—and why, 39–40

who uses our product/service
in unexpected ways, 41–43

Cutting Edge, The, 173

Daisy Rock Guitars, 192

Dancing with the Stars, 171

databases, 91

consulting firms, 175

institutionalizing your inventory of Right Questions, 175

Dave and Buster's restaurants, 19

Dell, Michael, 86

Dell Computer, 7, *55*, 194, 195
DeTeMobil, 7
Dreamworks SKG, 195
Drumline, 174
Dunst, Kirsten, 174
Dwight, John, 41

"Eager Sellers and Stony Buyers"
    (Gourville), 108
Eagles (rock music group), 47
eBay, 6, 7, 197
Einstein, Albert, 35
elenchus, 30
emotional states
    activation or arousal of, 115–16,
        117
    compartmentalizing your mind
        and, 118–20
    creativity and, 114–20
    enhanced cognitive flexibility
        and, 116
    hedonic tones, 115, 116
    neutralizing emotional over-
        head, 117–20
E-Plus, 7
evaluation. *See also* analysis in
    ideation; FedEx; Webvan
    Billion-Dollar Idea, 195–97
    creative performance and, 122
    of new ideas, 96–100
    performance review, contribu-
        tions to database as factor,
        175

performance review of creative
    employees, 160–64, 167
pink televisions idea, 189–90
using skill-grading criteria
    grid, 158–59, *159*, 161–62,
        167
eyeglasses, 194

Family Guy, 19
Farlowe, Chris, 188
fashion magazine, 71–72
    logic tree for, 81–82
FedEx
    Express, 180
    ZapMail, 86–87, 97, 100, 106,
        180, 189, 220n 1
feedback. *See also* evaluation
    dealing with "The Meltdown"
        and "The Blowup," 162–64
    "less is more" fallacy, 160–61
    overcoming reluctance to pro-
        vide, 160–64
    provided to participants of
        Brainstorming workshop,
        148–49
    using skill-grading criteria
        grid, 158–59, 161–62
film industry. *See also specific films*
    films from one idea, 173–74
    formula for profitable film,
        172–74
Forever Stamp, 25–26, 37
Foster, Richard, 32, 33, 106–7

Frantz, Don, 1, 2, 17
Freeplay (wind-up radio), 36

Games People Play: The Psychology of Human Relationships (Berne), 129–30
gasoline retailing business, 21–23
"Gas-to-You" business concept, 21–23, 101–12
  analytical stages of idea, 101–11
  outcome of idea, 111–12
Gateway Computer, 7
gift-buying, 63–68, 126
  giver-centric gifts, 67–68
  heartwarming gifts, 64–65
  hobbies and interest gifts, 65–66
  process reviewed, 68
  Right Questions for, 208–9
gingerbread houses, 24–25
Glee, 174
Golding, William, 188
Google, 6
Gourville, John, 108
Grove Park Inn, Asheville, North Carolina, 24–25
GuitarFreaks arcade game, 171
Guitar Hero video game, 171
Guitar Hero III video game, 171

Häagen-Dazs ice cream, 18–19, 37
Haier Corporation, 42
Harris, Jim, 5
Harrison, George, 187–88

Help!, 187
Hennessey, Beth, 121, 123
Hindman, James, 29–30
Home Depot, 6, 7, 186, 196
hotel business, 24–25
Humphries, Steve, 48–49

IBM PC, 5
"Idea Crushers," 141–42
  the Big Mouth, 141, 142
  the Boss, 141–42
  Subject Matter Expert, 141, 142
idea factory, 165–81
  codifying and communicating baseline standards, 167
  deliberately changing the formula, 179–80
  formal decision-making process needed, 167–69
  formalizing the ideation process, 166–69
  officially adopting Brainsteering process, 169
  reinventing the wheel, 180
  rejuvenating system periodically, 179–81
  reorganizing idea-generation team, 179
  Right Questions, expanding sources, 170–74
  Right Questions, institutionalizing inventory of (database), 175

Right Questions (*cont.*)
unhealthy patterns, avoiding,
176–79
idea request from hell, 128–30
lowering expectations and, 130
from Mr. WDYYB, 129–30
from "thought partner," 128–29
Inagaki, Satoshi, 40
Innovation S Curve, *32*, 32–34,
176, 191
Innovation: The Attacker's Advantage (Foster), 32, 106–7
Inside-the-Shell Electric Egg
Scrambler, 104
insurance industry, 41
automobile insurance innovation, 191–92
USAA, 46
Iomega Zip Drive, 196

James, Bill, 93
Japan Babyfood Assn., 40
jet engines, 24
Jiffy Lube, 28–30, 37, 194

Kay, Rob, 171
Kelley, Ed, 30
King of the Hill, 19
Konami Corporation, 171

L.A. Gear, 195
Lennon, John, 188
Lester, Richard, 187

literature: creating best-seller, 8
logic trees, 74–84, 155, 156,
176–78
alternative logic tree: materials cost differences based on
manufacturing variances, *78*
analysis of 92 feature stories in
People magazine, *177*
applications for, 82
finding a lower-priced product,
76–77
how might a company build
its business by modifying its
existing product, *79*
how might a company modify
its existing product to attract
new users, *80*
materials cost differences based
on consumption/scrap issues, 77
muffin varieties, *76*
no "universal" tree, 76–77
number of layers for, 82–83
sanity check, 80–81
story angles for a celebrity
event, 83–84, *84*
story angles for a fashion trend,
81, 81–82
Lord of the Flies (Golding), 188

Madison, James Craig, 25
Madonna, 180
magazine group: teaching creativity at, 151–52

Maguire, Gregory, 8
Make It or Break It, 174
Mannesmann, 7
McCartney, Paul, 187–88
McKinsey & Company, 3–4,
   167
  performance reviews, 167
  Z-1-4 company research, 5–6,
   185, 195
MECE (mutually exclusive [and]
  collectively exhaustive), 72–74
  logic trees, 74–84, 155, 156 (*see
   also* logic trees)
  non-MECE scheme for divid-
   ing a game board, *74*
  schemes for dividing a game
   board, *73*
Method acting, 8
MGM, 173
Mobilcom, 7
Mobilfunk, 7
*Moneyball: The Art of Winning an
  Unfair Game* (Beane), 93–94
motivation, intrinsic and extrinsic, 120–23, 221n 1
Murphy, Shane, 114
Murto, Bill, 5

Oakland A's, 93–94, 220n 4
Office Depot, 7
Omnitel, 7
optimizing your personal ideation performance, 113–30

Orange, 7
Osborn, Alex, 10, 134

parlor tricks (including contests),
  144–45
  team contest, 20
Peapod, 97
People magazine, 177–78
  analysis of 92 feature stories in
   (logic tree), *177*
Phelps, Michael, 44–45
Picasso, Pablo, 35
Piedmont A-11 Offense, 48-49
Plato, 30
Pollock, Jackson, 89–90
Pop Idol, 171
Priceline.com, 6, 195
Progressive Insurance, 41
  Snapshot, 192

R&D labs, 165
Reebok, 6
Reed, John, 95
retail sector
  catalog retailer, 165
  debt collection, 139–41
  self-checkout lanes in supermarkets, 46–47
Revenge of the Nerds, 173, 174
Revenge of the Nerds II, 173
Right Process, 4, 9–11
  analysis of ideas, 85–112
  vs. brainstorming, 9–11

Right Process (*cont.*)
giving Brainsteering workshops, 136–49
ideation sessions, number of Right Questions needed, 59–60
length of sessions, 124–25
tailoring the idea-generation process to your personal style, 123–28
teaching the approach to others, 156–57
time between sessions, 125–26
using MECE and logic trees, 72–84

Right Questions, 4–9, 17–84
ability to answer, 113–30
as "anchor" for thinking, 20–21
antiquity of approach, 30
best-question-used-before situation, 23–27
Billion-Dollar Idea and, 6, 12, 185–97
choosing the right questions from your arsenal, 53–60
database creation, 175
developing your arsenal, 31–51
exploring unexpected successes, 41–43
fields of application, 8–9
finding the perfect gift, 63–68
five lines of inquiry for, 37

four criteria for, 31–35
future needs as focus of, 51
"Gas-to-You" business concept, 21–23
genetic markers and, 50
imagining perfection, 43–47
institutional history, mining for within, 170
intuitive approach, 72
key obstacle focus, 35–36
limiting of conceptual space to be explored, 34
looking at other people's success and asking yourself what question led to it, 36–37
looking for *un*known patterns, 40
measured by success of, 34–35
multiple paths to the same great idea, 27–30
new perspective forced by, 31–33
number of ideas generated from, 143
providing multiple possibilities, 34
reusing the same questions, 127–28, 130
"soft" or "hard" ways, 192
sources for, 170–74
stealing best ideas of others, 170–72
stealing intellectual models of competitors, 172–75

systematic approach to developing, 71–84, 155

tailoring questions, 60–63, 139

Z-1-4 companies and, 5–6, 7

Right Questions: categories and prototypes, 76–77, 199–209

cost reduction ideas, 76–77, 77, 176, 204–8

customer-focused, 21–23, 25–27, 29, 37–47, 176, 199–203, 207

de-averaging users and activities, 39–41, 200–201

discovering unrecognized "headroom," 47–50, 202–3

"emotionally powerful as a child/expensive form for adults" question, 18–19, 37, 124, 146–47

exploring unexpected successes, 41–43, 201–2

finding the perfect gift, 63–68, 126, 208–9

imagining perfection, 202

insurance industry, 191–92

new products and services, 199–203

product distribution, 192–93

sales efforts, boosting, 203–4

signpost examples, 28, 63, 64–67, 68

"Who has a significant need for this kind of product . . . ," 35–36, 200

Right Questions: choosing the best from your arsenal, 53–60, 68

example: finding the perfect gift, 63–68

four tests for each question, 54–59

information is available to answer the question, 57

number of, and number of ideation sessions, 59–60

prompts ideas the organization will embrace (vs. major changes in status quo), 57–59

right balance of question types for portfolio of choices, 59

suggests directions that fit your specific current needs, 56–57

targets an aspect that has received little past attention or forces a significantly different perspective, 54–56

Rollerblades, 18–19, 37

sabermetrics, 93–94

sanity check, 35, 80–81, 189–90

signpost examples, 28, 63, 68

finding the perfect gift, 64–67

Simpsons, The, 19

Sinyard, Mike, 37–38

skill-grading criteria, 158–59, *159*, 161–62, 167

Skype video-telephony, 66

Snuggie, 104

"Social Psychology of Creativity, The" (Hennessey), 121, 123

Socratic method, 30

sounding board, 126–27

Specialized Bike Components, 37–38

Spinelli, Stephen, 28, 30

sports
  Arena Football League, 113
  Berkoff Blastoff, 44–45
  Oakland A's, 93–94, 220n 4
  Piedmont A-11 Offense, 48–49
  sabermetrics, 93–94
  ultimate fighting, 8–9

Staples, 7, 195

Strictly Come Dancing, 171

systematic approach to developing questions, 71–84
  logic trees, 74–84, *76*, *77*, *78*, *79*, *80*, *81*
  MECE, 72–74, *73*, *74*

tailoring questions, 60–63, 139

Tata, Ratan and the Tata Group, 55–56

Tata Nano, 55–56

technology
  analysis in ideation: showstoppers, 105–6
  computer retailers, 7, 55

fax machines, 87

laptop computers, 4–5, 6, 7, 17, 35, 54

length of time before society fully capitalizes on major new technologies, 49

software to simplify computer use, 38–39

Z-1-4 companies, 7

television news, 153–55

television shows, 88–89
  American copies of British shows, 171
  Hollywood as originator of, 171
  idea factory and, 165
  "reunion" magazine features, 178

"thinking outside the box" fallacy, 21, 34, 133, 137

'Til Death Us Do Part, 171

Tito, Dennis, 19

Touchstone Pictures, 174

Toys R Us, 7

traveler's checks, 42–43

Twentieth Century Fox, 173, 174

Ultimate Fighting Championship I, 8–9

unhealthy patterns, 31–34, 176–79
  Innovation S Curve, *32*, 32–34, 176

United Technologies, 24, 25

Universal Studios, 173

"unrecognized headroom" Right
    Questions, 47–50, 202–3
    where are we operating under a
        set of rules that need reexam-
        ining, 49
    where do the "rules" already pro-
        vide more flexibility . . . , 47–49
    which technologies underlying
        our production and operating
        processes have changed most,
        50
USAA, 46
U.S. Postal Service, 25–26

vending machines, 45–46
Virgin Atlantic, 27
VisionSpring, 194

Walt Disney Company, 174
Web designers, 165
Webvan, 97–100, 106, 189
Who Wants to Be a Millionaire?, 171
*Wicked: The Life and Times of
    the Wicked Witch of the West*
    (Maguire), 8

"Yesterday" (McCartney),
    187–88

Z-1-4 companies, 5–6, 12, 17, 55,
    185
    average investment to start,
        186
    Billion-Dollar Idea for,
        185–97
    chart: core ideas and potential
        Right Questions, 7
    companies that achieved a
        three-year jump on competi-
        tors, 196
    companies that offered dramat-
        ically lower prices, 195
    companies that "reinvented" an
        entire category of products,
        196–97
    multiple paths to the same
        great idea, 27–30
    near Z-1-4 companies, 6
    single concept basis of, 6,
        195
zone ("in the zone"), 114

About the Authors

Kevin P. Coyne is a senior teaching professor at the Goizueta Business School at Emory University and a former senior partner and leader of the worldwide strategy practice at McKinsey & Company. His articles have appeared in the *Harvard Business Review*, *McKinsey Quarterly*, *Sloan Management Review*, and other leading publications, and on Business-Week.com. He has been featured throughout the media, including the *Wall Street Journal*, *New York Times*, *Financial Times*, *Fortune*, CNBC, National Public Radio, and Fox Business News.

Shawn T. Coyne is a management consultant with twenty-five years of experience in strategy, marketing, and organizational leadership at Procter & Gamble, McKinsey & Company, and other leading firms. He has authored or coauthored articles for the *Harvard Business Review*, *Executive Decision*, and BusinessWeek.com, and he has appeared in the *Wall Street Journal* and on Fox Business News.

Kevin and Shawn are the managing directors of The Coyne Partnership, a boutique consulting firm serving senior executives and boards of directors in both the private and public sectors in the areas of strategy, innovation, and organizational effectiveness.